Ph...

Gern...

(from The Kennel...

Tail: High set, curled right up from root, lying curled over back.

Body: Length from point of shoulder to point of buttock equal to height at withers; short, well-developed loin. Moderate tuck-up. Well ribbed up and rounded. Top-line level.

Hindquarters: Moderate angulation with hocks moderately well let down.

Coat: Double coat consisting of a soft woolly undercoat and a long harsh-textured perfectly straight top coat covering the whole of the body. Tail profusely covered with long spreading hair.

Size: Height:
Klein: 23–29 cms (9–11.5 ins)
Mittel: 30–38 cms (12–15 ins).

Feet: Small, rounded, cat-like, with well arched toes.

Coventry C

German Spitz

By Juliette Cunliffe

Contents

PUBLISHED IN THE UNITED KINGDOM BY:

INTERPET
PUBLISHING

Vincent Lane, Dorking, Surrey RH4 3YX England

ISBN 1-84286-019-4

Photography by Carol Ann Johnson and Michael Trafford with additional photographs by:

Norvia Behling, TJ Calhoun, Carolina Biological Supply, Doskocil, Isabelle Francais, James Hayden-Yoav, James R Hayden, RBP, Bill Jonas, Dwight R Kuhn, Dr Dennis Kunkel, Mikki Pet Products, Phototake, Jean Claude Revy, Dr Andrew Spielman and Alice van Kempen.

Owner credits: The publisher would like to thank Pat Hawker, Audrey Metcalfe and Carol Westwood for allowing their dogs to be photographed for this book.

The sizes recognised in the UK as German Spitz are the Klein and the Mittel. This is an adult black German Spitz Mittel.

History of the
GERMAN SPITZ

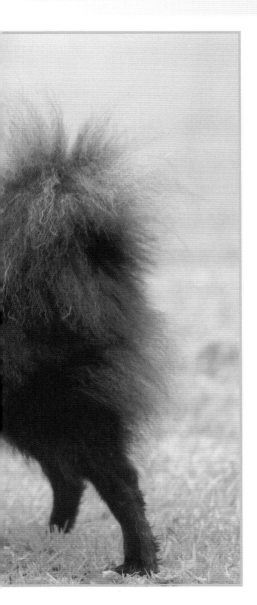

The German Spitz has a long history, because, as a member of the European spitz group of dogs, its ancestors can be traced back to the hunter-gatherers of the Stone Age some 6000 years ago. However, without delving too far back into the mists of time but rather bringing us closer to the present day, we need to go back to the Turf Spitz. This was a dog that was buried by accident and preserved in the peat bogs ranging from the northern plain of Germany through most of Denmark. Because this was an area of swampland, houses were built on stilts and, over time, well-preserved humans and dogs have been recovered from the resultant peat bogs.

It is generally believed that the dogs found were the ancestors of the German Spitz, and it is thought that the hunting instinct had been deliberately bred out of them because house dogs and herders were of more use than hunting dogs to these non-nomadic peoples. Of greater importance was that they would stay near the homestead and give voice when intruders approached.

Another theory is that white coats were favoured, for this

would allow the dogs to be distinguished easily from marauding wolves and thus prevent them from being killed accidentally. It should be stressed, however, that the hunting instinct's being bred out and the preference for the colour white remain only as theories and are by no means proven.

What we do know for sure is that they were good watchdogs of the old-fashioned kind, protecting not only farms but also vineyards, warehouses, barges, wagons and peddlers' packs. This is a member of a group of breeds that has always been ready to give voice,

and one that was given the name of *mistbeller*, which can be translated as 'dung-hill barker.'

The spitz dogs developed rather differently in various countries, doing such things as running alongside coaches or riding on the backs of horses. They varied both in size and in colour, for selective breeding has always taken place, as indeed it has with all domestic animals.

During the 18th century, the breed started to gain popularity in England, for George I came to the throne in 1714. His wife was German, and the couple's descendants also married German aristo-

The dog known as the German Wolf Spitz is akin to the Keeshond of Holland.

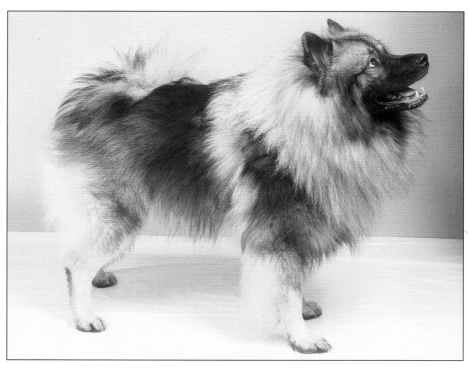

we know as the Pomeranian today.

It is quite remarkable how a dog that had been essentially a peasant's dog became so highly favoured by royalty and the upper classes. Queen Charlotte, the German wife of King George III, brought two Pomeranians, Phoebe (also spelt Phebe) and Mercury, to Britain in 1767. Here they lived in Kew, West London, as did the artist Gainsborough, who came regularly into contact with the breed through his work. These dogs were featured prominently in the works of famous artists, notably Gainsborough and Stubbs. It was the fashion of the day to

Thomas Gainsborough's *Pomeranian and Puppy*.

crats, giving rise to many German visitors to the English court. With them they brought their dogs, and it was these that were effectively the forerunners of today's German Spitz. The dogs were known then as Pomeranians and were believed to have originated in a place called Pomerania (Pommern), a former duchy on the Baltic, between eastern Germany and western Poland. These dogs were considerably larger than the breed

SPITZ DOGS
The word 'spitz' is a general word used to describe dogs with pointed ears and sharp muzzles. They all have curled tails and dense, double coats. In Britain, the Pomeranian, German Spitz (Klein and Mittel) and Keeshond are just four of many spitz breeds.

GENUS *CANIS*
Dogs and wolves are members of the genus *Canis*. Wolves are known scientifically as *Canis lupus* while dogs are known as *Canis domesticus*. Dogs and wolves are known to interbreed. The term *canine* derives from the Latin-derived word *Canis*. The term 'dog' has no scientific basis but has been used for thousands of years. The origin of the word 'dog' has never been authoritatively ascertained.

a lady who did much to bring the public's attention to pedigree dogs. She became deeply involved with this breed and imported dogs varying in weight between 3 and 7 pounds. Indeed one of Queen Victoria's Pomeranians, Gona, was among the first of the breed to win a prize at a British dog show. Her Majesty had first come into contact with the breed when she

Pomeranian and girl depicted on an ancient Athenian wine jug from the fourth century BC.

have one's portrait painted to include a favourite pet. Today, by seeing paintings of that time in which a dog was portrayed alongside its owner, we can obtain a rough idea of the dog's size. Several paintings include white dogs, but one of special note was that of 'Fino,' a black and white parti-colour.

Queen Victoria's Marco, from a photograph by Russell and Sons.

Queen Victoria, a grand-daughter of Queen Charlotte, was

travelled to Italy in 1888 and obtained several dogs in Florence. Among these was Marco, who weighed 5.5 kgs (12 lbs) and with whom she achieved notable success at shows, including Crufts.

A great lover of many different kinds of dogs, Queen Victoria owned a kennel of Pomeranians, bred under the prefix 'Windsor.' There is rather an amusing story of an instance when Her Majesty wished to exhibit three Pomeranians of a colour not usually shown in England. A special class was provided for her exhibits, and two of them were lucky enough to be awarded joint first prize! So much did Queen Victoria love the breed that even when she was dying, her Pomeranian, Turi, was always on her bed.

A prominent figure in the world of dogs, Charles Henry Lane was invited to inspect Her Majesty's kennels. He spoke highly of the dogs' circumstances, as every care and consideration

WORK OF ART

The famous artist Gainsborough is one of several who often portrayed Pomeranians in his paintings. In London's Wallace Collection, there is a particularly famous painting of the actress, Mrs Robinson, who has a large white Pomeranian sitting by her side.

Although dogs descended from wolves, the German Spitz's Pomeranian relative is required to have a 'fox' head. Shown here is the adult kit fox.

were being shown for their happiness. He described the spitz dogs primarily as what he termed

A drawing entitled 'A Black Pomeranian' from Vero Shaw's *Book of the Dog.*

one could purchase. This said, supply soon overtook demand and the breed dropped rapidly in value.

A great deal of in-breeding was going on at that time and some signs of degeneration were evident, such as a tendency toward apple heads in smaller-sized specimens, something quite out of keeping with the fox-headed requirement of the breed.

Aided in part by Queen Victoria's prominence and people's consequent interest in the breed, the English Kennel Club officially recognised the Pomeranian in 1870 and the Pomeranian Club drew up the first English breed standard in 1891.

The range of sizes among the various spitz dogs was very considerable and, as in so many breeds, miniaturisation was favoured, both in Britain and the rest of Europe. In Europe, the dogs of this kind were divided into five separate breeds; Wolf Spitz, which was the colour of a Keeshond but larger in size; the Large Spitz, of Keeshond size but of various colours; the Medium Spitz, akin to our German Spitz Mittel; the Small Spitz, like our German Spitz Klein; and finally the Dwarf Spitz, which was equivalent to Britain's Pomeranian.

In Britain, the name Pomeranian was retained. Although there were no height restrictions, there were divisions

'off-colours,' although some were exceedingly pretty. Although some were somewhat larger, most were what he called 'small-medium.'

Mr Gladstone was another prominent person who was much taken by the breed and is said to have owned a black Pomeranian. As the 20th century turned, there was a saying, 'there's money in Poms,' for they were selling for up to £250; so, ounce for ounce, Pomeranians were probably the most expensive breed of dog that

The Large Spitz
(German Gross
Spitz) has never
been as numerous
as the Dwarf Spitz
or Pomeranian.

according to weight, and these changed as the years went by. In 1889, a division was made at 10 pounds, but by 1896 it had become 8 pounds. Then, early in the 20th century, a new standard was drawn up with the dividing line at 7 pounds, with the larger dogs being called Pomeranians and the smaller dogs being called Pomeranian Miniatures. As time moved on, interest in the larger dogs waned, and by 1909 dogs were required to weigh 3–4 lbs, with bitches larger than the males at 5–6 lbs. It was important that the bitches be a bit larger, as this was of assistance in breeding.

However, larger dogs had been bred and they did not die out overnight; thus, bigger specimens certainly appeared from time to time. Although they were kept as pets rather than as show dogs, the larger bitches were useful to breed from, for they did not encounter such complications at whelping time.

In 1904, it was written, 'There is no species of ladies' pet-dog that has achieved such universal popularity in so short a time as the Pomeranian.' Early in the 20th century, several prominent people in dogs expressed their views on the breed. According to Mrs Hamilton, who regularly took top honours in the breed, her ideal Pomeranian was 'a bright little creature, sparkling all over with life and fun, devoted to his master or mistress, and sharing all their joys and sorrows as much as lies in a doggy's power.' Mrs Hamilton said that she had come across many of the breed that had been almost human in their keenness of perception and had expressed the utmost sympathy during times when their owners were distressed. She thought them as clever at tricks as Poodles, and, though excitable by nature, they never allow their anger to get the better of their discretion.

DEVELOPMENT IN RECENT DECADES
In the early 1970s, Pomeranian enthusiast Averil Cawthera decided that she wished to establish the white Pomeranian, so in 1975 imported Tum Tum van het Vlinderhof of Lireva ('Tum-Tum') a white dog from Holland, with a black bitch, Venestein's Mauricia of Lireva ('Velvet'), following in 1976.

Shortly after Averil Cawthera had imported the black and white dogs from Holland, Rosemary Bridgeman bought a fairly oversized Pomeranian, April Folly at Tordown, and she, along with Janet Al-Haddad, made serious endeavours to get the larger Spitz recognised. In effect, the larger-sized Pomeranian and the Klein Spitz were the very same, so these two ladies tried to get them recognised as 'Victorian Pomeranians,' a charming name and thoroughly evocative in view of Her Majesty's love of the breed.

Later, Averil Cawthera's Dutch dogs, Tum Tum and Velvet, were purchased by Rosemary Bridgeman in 1977 and 1978, respectively. Then, in 1979, Mmes Al-Haddad and Bridgeman, along with Julie Smith, imported a Dutch bitch, Tefanra-Leona's Lady Xabrina, fondly known as 'Minty.'

It was at this time that confusion arose over registered breed names. Minty had been registered in Holland under the name of 'Kleine Keeshond,' but her English Kennel Club registration just referred to her as a Keeshond, which she was certainly not! It was believed that Tum-Tum and Minty had been registered as Klein Keeshonden, but, as it later transpired, this had not been the case. The Kennel Club then changed Minty's breed registration to 'Pomeranian,' but by this time she had already been entered at a show as a Kleine Keeshond. This was all very confusing indeed!

In 1981, Janet Al-Haddad imported a white Klein Spitz from Frau Pinner in Vienna. This was Prinz Schneeflocke von Cottas, who was also included here on the Pomeranian register. It perhaps comes as no great surprise that there was enormous opposition from Pomeranian breeders, and it was considered that the larger spitz would stand a

A pair of German Spitz Klein. Klein in German means 'small.'

greater chance of succeeding as a breed if all reference to the Pomeranian was dropped. It was therefore decided that a breed club should be formed, and that a separate breed, German Spitz, should be aimed for, with the intention of having it included in the Utility Group rather than in the Toy Group.

On, 3 February 1982, the inaugural meeting of the German Spitz Club took place at the Bantam Pub at Burghfield Common, the home of Bob and Chris Trendle, who were much involved in the breed in its early years. Rosemary Bridgeman was President and Janet Al-Haddad (then Edmonds) was Chairman, with Pat Mais in the post of Secretary.

Confusion over breed registration names began to raise its ugly head, for there were only two dogs that had 'correct' registrations.

However, The Kennel Club could see that devotees of the larger spitz were not going to give up, and, with help from Mike Stockman, it was agreed that Tum-Tum and Velvet also be included in the genetic pool, and their progeny as well, if their owners so wished.

For transference onto the German Spitz register, offspring had to have one of the original four imports in the pedigree, but this decision was to be made by the owner, not by the breeder, and application for registration had to be made with six months. Obviously pure offspring from the dogs that had become known as the 'First Four' went straight onto the full register, but there was a development register for others.

FIRST CC

The first set of Challenge Certificates was awarded to a German Spitz at Crufts in 1995. The judge was Chris Trendle, of the Lusam affix, at whose pub the German Spitz Club's inaugural meeting was held in 1982.

It was also necessary to decide upon the two sizes of German Spitz, and The Kennel Club said that they should be known as 'Mittel' and 'Klein,' their reason being that these names would supposedly cause less confusion than the English words 'Standard' and 'Miniature.' Owners were to decide upon the size registered, but, once registered, there was to be no interbreeding between the

Determined solely by their inches, German Spitzen are divided into Klein and Mittel varieties.

The white German Spitz, similar to the Volpino of Italy and the American Eskimo, is a popular and attractive coloration.

two. To decide which dogs were to be registered as Klein and which as Mittel, the dogs were measured, but this understandably resulted in siblings, especially of different sexes, being registered as two different sizes.

The early breeders of German Spitz were willing to allow any colour and markings within the breed, and this was looked upon positively by The Kennel Club. This makes for great and spectacular variety, but can present a slight problem in defining colour when registering puppies, for the colours of German Spitzen often changes with maturity. This means that a youngster may be registered as one particular colour, but can all too easily turn out to

be a rather different colour!

In 1995, Challenge Certificate status was awarded to the breed, this only ten years after its recognition by England's Kennel Club. The breed club was sensible enough to clarify and alter certain

The Keeshond exhibits the colour of the German Wolf Spitz.

details within the breed standard before the permanent standard was put into place.

IN THE USA

Sadly, the German Spitz is not particularly popular in the USA, but the Pomeranian, Keeshond and American Eskimo Dogs, which are related breeds, find greater favour there. The American Eskimo, a breed as yet unknown in the UK, is a compactly built white dog that was popular with circus performers in the 20th century. This breed, which was recognised by the American Kennel Club in 1994, is divided into three sizes,

THE STAMP OF RECOGNITION

Over the years, the German Spitz has often been depicted on postage stamps, cigarette cards and trade cards from several parts of the world. Russia, Austria, Germany, Britain, the USA and even the State of Oman have all thought the breed worthy of representation in this way. George Stubbs' painting of Fino and Tiny has been depicted on stamps in the USA and in Britain.

the smallest from 9 to 12 inches (23 to 30.5 cms), and the largest 15 to 19 inches (38 to 48 cms).

Another close spitz relative, the American Eskimo Dog, is quite popular in the United States.

A dwarf pony and its rider, a German Spitz. While not well-known worldwide, this spirited spitz charmer has won the hearts and devotion of a dedicated following.

Bold, confident and intelligent, the German Spitz possesses an happy nature and zest for life that show in his delightful expression.

Characteristics of the
GERMAN SPITZ

MEET THE GERMAN SPITZ
The German Spitz is bright, confident and lively, with a certain boldness and adventurous spirit. Small in size, this is an intelligent breed, and thus needs plenty to keep its mind well occupied. This attractive little breed is well suited to most home environments, but it should be borne in mind that it is a heavily coated dog that will need regular grooming.

The German Spitz has a fairly independent nature and, like many members of the spitz family, does have a tendency to be noisy, though this can usually be controlled with sensible training. The reason that they can be rather noisy is that they are highly alert little guard dogs, and their natural instinct is to bark when they find themselves in new or alarming situations.

PERSONALITY
An happy, light-hearted dog, the German Spitz is devoted to its family; indeed, this is stated as a characteristic of the breed in its standard of perfection. It has an even, confident disposition—such an intelligent, adventurous personality inside a canine frame can simply never be ignored—but should show no sign of either nervousness or aggression.

The German Spitz usually enjoys the company of other people, and of dogs and other household pets, but, as with most breeds, should be socialised while developing its personality as a youngster.

THE COMPANY OF CHILDREN
Whether or not any dog will get on well with children depends very much on the child's upbringing and sensible parental control. This is a breed that enjoys the company of humans, and children are of course included, and German Spitzen will readily join in with family games.

However, young children and dogs should always be supervised when together, for although the breed is not large enough to pull or knock over a child, it is small enough that the child might harm the dog, albeit inadvertently. The coat can be pulled, and toddlers often can be quite rough in their games, so they must be taught to treat dogs kindly, gently and respectfully.

clearly described in the breed standard.

Ears are covered with soft, short hair, but the hair on the face is smooth and short. The lovely curled tail is covered with long spreading hair that is profuse and makes a fine picture.

It is of the utmost importance to understand that this is absolutely not a trimmed breed. German Spitz should never be clipped, even if an owner might think this sensible for a pet during the hot summer months. This is because clipping the coat causes it to lose its insulating properties, so such action may well have the opposite effect to that intended!

Tidying the coat is a different matter, and this is usually done on the feet, the anal area and the legs below the hocks, but certainly nowhere else.

This Klein bitch beautifully displays the breed's abundant coat and magnificent curled tail.

DID YOU KNOW?

At the first sign of any minor infection, breeders have found that live yoghurt, administered orally, is of great benefit. This sometimes has the effect of rectifying the problem almost immediately, before a course of antibiotics becomes necessary.

COLOUR

Any breed that comes in a wide variety of colours makes an attractive sight in the show ring, but the German Spitz has to create one of the most spectacular of such sights. All colour varieties and markings are acceptable. Having said this, the most predominant colours are black and gold. Black and tan is only occasionally seen, but wolf sable, black and white parti-colours, blues and creams are among the variety of hues that can be found.

HEALTH CONSIDERATIONS

In general, the German Spitz is a fairly healthy little breed, and certainly it encounters far fewer problems than many others. However, certain health issues can arise, so it is in the best interests of the breed to know what to look out for. If owners are aware of the problems that can occur, they are undoubtedly in a position to deal with them in the best manner possible. Some problems are genetic and are carried via

A veritable Spitz Klein rainbow, representing but a fraction of the shades and combinations possible in this splendidly colourful breed.

WEIGHT WATCHER

Elderly dogs can sometimes be prone to putting on excess weight. The profuse coat of a German Spitz can all too often deceive an owner into thinking that the dog is of correct weight, when in fact it is too fat. Over-eating or feeding the wrong foods may be the cause. Often an older dog requires a slightly different diet from a younger one.

heredity, but others are not.

When the standard of the German Spitz was drawn up, any exaggerated features that might lead to health problems were sensibly avoided, thus undoubtedly help to produce a generally robust, active breed.

LUXATING PATELLA

Some German Spitz suffer from trouble with the knee joints, known as luxating patella. It is prudent when selecting a puppy to chose one whose parents have both been certified clear of patellar luxation. This is a problem that is fairly common among small breeds; the German Spitz's close relative, the tiny Pomeranian, can also suffer from this. This can occur in both sizes of German Spitzen.

Many dogs with luxating patella live with it without experiencing pain, in part because the breed is fairly light in weight. However, surgery sometimes has to be resorted to in severe cases.

DID YOU KNOW?

To take a urine sample to your veterinary surgeon for analysis, the easiest way is to catch the urine in a large, clean bowl and then transfer it into a bottle. An owner attempting to get his dog or bitch to urinate directly into a bottle will spend many fruitless hours in his efforts!

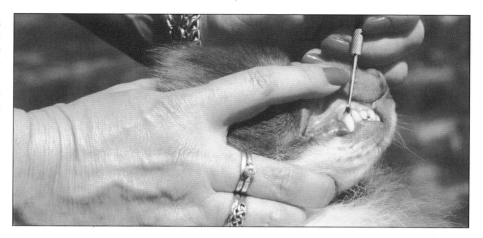

It is sensible to train your German Spitz not to do any strenuous jumping, especially from high places, for this can result in damage to the knees. Climbing up and down stairs should ideally also be restricted or, at the least, supervised. Another important factor is that a dog should not be overweight, as this is likely to exacerbate the problem.

Teeth

It is important to pay close attention to the care of teeth and gums so that they remain as healthy as possible, thereby preventing decay, infection and resultant loss. As with many other small breeds, some German Spitzen lose their teeth at a relatively early age.

If a gum infection is evident, always deal with it promptly, for the infection may not just stop at the gums. The bacteria can be carried through the bloodstream, the result of which can be disease of the liver, kidneys, heart and joints. This is all the more reason to realise that efficient dental care is of utmost importance throughout a dog's life.

Feeding dried foods is recommended by many as a means of helping to keep teeth clean and in good condition, but, of course, regular careful brushing with a veterinary toothpaste can help enormously.

Another dental problem to be aware of is retention of deciduous teeth, meaning that a puppy's baby teeth may not drop out on their own. Should they still be in place when the adult teeth begin to develop, it is worth taking your puppy to the vet to see if they need extraction. If the baby teeth remain in place when the new teeth come through, they will push the adult teeth out of alignment. This is something that can be a problem in Pomeranians, and with Pomeranians so close in the breed's ancestry it is wise to keep this mind.

EYE INFECTIONS

Always be sure to keep a careful check on the cleanliness and condition of your German Spitz's eyes, so as to avoid eye infections' arising. At the first sign of injury, especially if the eye is starting to turn blue in colour, urgent veterinary attention is required. Early diagnosis and treatment can often save a dog's sight.

HEART PROBLEMS

Occasionally dogs can suffer from heart problems, particularly as they become more advanced in age. It is therefore sensible to request your vet to check the dog's heart whenever visiting the surgery for routine examination or vaccination, though many good vets will do this automatically.

KIDNEY STONES

Kidney stones can occur in many breeds and may appear in either sex. However, because the urethra of the male is longer and narrower than that of the female, obstruction is more common in males.

Symptoms of kidney stones are frequent urination, bloody urine, dribbling urine, straining, weakness, depression, vomiting and pain, so it is evident that urgent veterinary advice should be sought. Although kidney stones can occur in puppies even less than two months old, they usually appear in adults between two and ten years old.

DOGS, DOGS, GOOD FOR YOUR HEART!

People usually purchase dogs for companionship, but studies show that dogs can help to improve their owners' health and level of activity, as well as lower a human's risk of coronary heart disease. Without even realising it, when a person puts time into exercising, grooming and feeding a dog, he also puts more time into his own personal health care. Dog owners establish more routine schedules for their dogs to follow, which can have positive effects on a human's health. Dogs also teach us patience, offer unconditional love and provide the joy of having a furry friend to pet!

Best in Show winner at a German Spitz club show. Dogs on the Continent are compared to the breed standard set forth by the FCI (Fédération Cynologique Internationale).

Breed Standard for the
GERMAN SPITZ

INTRODUCTION TO THE BREED STANDARD

The breed standard for the German Spitz is set down by The Kennel Club and, like standards for other breeds, can be changed occasionally. Such changes come about usually with guidance from experienced people from within the breed clubs, but it should be understood that, in Britain, The Kennel Club has the final word as to what is incorporated and in what manner. The first standard drawn up for this breed was an interim standard, but now the official German Spitz standard is in place, the only difference between the Klein and Mittel being that of size.

It is perhaps of interest to note that, in the interim standard, the heights were a little different from what they are now. Kleins had a height of 23–28 cms (9–11 ins) and Mittels were from 29–35.5 cms (11.5–14 ins), hence both with a smaller height allowance than that of today's standard. Also, today the breed standard calls only for dogs to be masculine and bitches feminine, whereas in the interim standard dogs preferably were to be larger than bitches. With such a range within the sizes, it is understandable that some larger bitches will weigh more than some smaller dogs, thus the standard omitted this requirement.

Such changes, however minor they may appear, go to show how beneficial it is for a new or newly developed breed to have time with an interim standard before a fully approved standard is put into effect.

All breed standards are designed effectively to paint a picture in words, though each reader will almost certainly have a slightly different way of interpreting these words. After all, were everyone to interpret a breed's standard in exactly the same way, there would only be one consistent winner within the breed at any given time!

In any event, to fully comprehend the intricacies of a breed, reading words alone is never enough. In addition, it is essential for devotees to watch German Spitzen being judged at shows and, if possible, to attend seminars at which the breed is discussed. This enables owners to absorb as much as possible about this particular breed of dog. 'Hands on' experience, providing an opportunity to assess the structure of dogs, is always valuable, especially for those who hope ultimately to breed or judge the German Spitz.

A breed standard undoubtedly helps breeders to produce stock that comes as close as possible to the recognised standard; likewise, it helps judges to know exactly what they are looking for. This enables each judge to make a carefully considered decision when selecting the most typical specimen present to head his line of winners.

However familiar one is with the German Spitz, it is always worth refreshing one's memory by re-reading the standard, for it is sometimes all too easy to overlook, or perhaps conveniently forget, certain features.

THE KENNEL CLUB STANDARD FOR THE GERMAN SPITZ

General Appearance: Compact, short-coupled and well knit with an almost square outline. Firm condition, the profuse coat not disguising any lack of substance.

Characteristics: The German Spitz is intelligent, active and alert. Its buoyancy, independence and devotion to the family are the breed characteristics.

Temperament: Happy, equable disposition, showing confidence, with no sign of nervousness or aggression.

Head and Skull: Medium large, broad and nearly flat skull when viewed from above and narrowing in a wedge shape to the nose. Stop moderately defined; muzzle approximately half length of head. Cheeks clean. Flews tight, no trace of lippiness.

Nose: Black in blacks, whites, black/white parti-colours, black/tan bi-colours. Self colour as compatible with coat colour in other colour varieties. Never parti-colour or pink.

Eyes: Medium size, oval-shaped and obliquely set. Not too wide apart. Always dark with black rims in blacks, whites, black/white parti-colours, black/tan bi-colours. As dark as compatible with coat colour in other colour varieties.

Ears: Small, triangular and set rather high. Perfectly erect.

Mouth: A perfect, regular and complete scissor bite, i.e. upper teeth closely overlapping lower teeth and set square to the jaws. Black lips in blacks, whites, black/white parti-colours, black/tan bi-colours. Colours as compatible with coat colour in other colour varieties.

Neck: Clean, moderately short and well set into the shoulders.

Forequarters: Moderately sloping shoulder; upper arm of sufficient length to ensure elbow is vertically below point of withers. Moderate forechest. Elbows equidistant between ground and withers, turning neither in nor out. Well-boned, straight legs. Pasterns strong and flexible.

Body: Length from point of shoulder to point of buttock equal to height at withers; short, well-developed loin. Moderate tuck-up. Well ribbed up and rounded. Distance from brisket to ground not less than half the height from ground to withers. Topline level.

Hindquarters: Moderate angulation with hocks moderately well let down. Neither cow-hocked nor wide behind.

Feet: Small, rounded, cat-like, with well arched toes.

Tail: High set, curled right up from root, lying curled over back.

Gait/Movement: Moving without exaggeration from any angle. Straight coming and going. Viewed from side, effortless, brisk action, retaining topline.

Coat: Double coat consisting of a soft woolly undercoat and a long harsh-textured perfectly straight top coat covering the whole of the body. Very abundant around neck and forequarters with a frill of profuse off-standing straight hair extending over the shoulders. Forelimbs well feathered tapering from elbows to pasterns. Hindlimbs feathered to hocks. Ears covered with soft short hair. Hair on the face smooth and short. Tail profusely covered with long spreading hair. This is not a trimmed breed and evidence of trimming and shaping, other than tidying of the feet, anal area and legs below the hocks, unacceptable.

Colour: All colour varieties and markings acceptable. Butterfly pigment not permitted with any colour.

Size: Height: Klein: 23–29 cms (9–11.5 ins). Mittel: 30–38 cms (12–15 ins). Dogs masculine, bitches feminine.

Faults: Any departure from the foregoing points should be considered a fault and the seriousness with which the fault should be regarded should be in exact proportion to its degree.

Note: Male animals should have two apparently normal testicles fully descended into the scrotum.

GERMAN SPITZ

OWNER CONSIDERATIONS

Before reaching the decision that you will begin your search for a German Spitz puppy, it is essential that you are fully clear in your mind that this is absolutely the most suitable breed for you and for your family. You should have carefully researched the breed prior to making the important decision that a German Spitz should join you and your family in its daily life.

When you have made that decision, you must also ask yourself why you want a German Spitz: do you want one purely as a pet or as a show dog? This should be made clear to the breeder when you make your initial enquiries. If looking for a show dog, you will certainly need to take the breeder's advice as to which available puppy shows the most promise for the show ring. If looking for a pet, you should discuss your family situation with the breeder and take his advice as to which puppy is likely to suit best.

When you have your first opportunity to visit the most potentially suitable litter, watch the puppies interact together. You will find that different puppies have different personalities, and some will be more boisterous and extroverted than others. You should expect the puppies to come to you, even if they don't know you, so don't take pity on the unduly shy puppy that sits quietly in a corner. Although you will need to use your own judgement as to which one is most likely to fit in with your own lifestyle, if the breeder you have selected is a good one, you will also gain much from his knowledge and guidance.

You should have done plenty of research on the breed, and preferably have visited at least one of the German Spitz club's breed shows or a Championship Show where the breed is scheduled with a separate classification, thus giving you an opportunity to see the German Spitz in some numbers. Such a visit will also provide you with a chance to see the dogs with their breeders, handlers and owners, and to ask questions. Provided you approach them when they are not terribly busy with the dogs, most are more than willing to answer questions, recommend breeders and give advice.

Remember that the German

Spitz you select should remain with you for the duration of its life, which hopefully will be around 13 years, so making the right decision from the outset is of utmost importance. No dog should be moved from one home to another simply because its owners were thoughtless enough not to have done sufficient 'homework' before selecting the breed. It is always important to remember that, when looking for a puppy, a good breeder will be assessing you as a prospective new owner just a carefully as you are selecting the breeder.

Puppies almost invariably look enchanting, but you must select one from a caring breeder who has given the puppies all the attention they deserve and has looked after them well. The puppy you select should look well-fed but not pot-bellied, as

YOUR SCHEDULE . . .
If you lead an erratic, unpredictable life, with daily or weekly changes in your work requirements, consider the problems of owning a puppy. The new puppy has to be fed regularly, socialised (loved, petted, handled, introduced to other people) and, most importantly, allowed to visit outdoors for toilet training. As the dog gets older, it can be more tolerant of deviations in its feeding and toilet relief.

HANDLE WITH CARE
You should be extremely careful about handling tiny puppies. Not that you might hurt them, but that the pups' mother may exhibit what is called 'maternal aggression.' It is a natural, instinctive reaction for the dam to protect her young against anything she interprets as predatory or possibly harmful to her pups.

The sweetest, most gentle of bitches, after whelping a litter, often reacts this way, even to her owner.

this might indicate worms. Eyes should look bright and clear, without discharge. The nose should be moist, an indication of good health, but should never be runny. It goes without saying that there should certainly be no evidence of loose motions, nor of parasites. Always check the bite

PREPARING FOR PUP

Unfortunately, when a puppy is bought by someone who does not take into consideration the time and attention that dog ownership requires, it is the puppy who suffers when he is either abandoned or placed in a shelter by a frustrated owner. So all of the 'homework' you do in preparation for your pup's arrival will benefit you both. The more informed you are, the more you will know what to expect and the better equipped you will be to handle the ups and downs of raising a puppy. Hopefully, everyone in the household is willing to do his part in raising and caring for the pup. The anticipation of owning a dog often brings a lot of promises from excited family members: 'I will walk him every day,' 'I will feed him,' 'I will house-train him,' etc., but these things take time and effort, and promises can easily be forgotten once the novelty of the new pet has worn off.

of your selected puppy to be sure that it is neither overshot nor undershot. This may not be too noticeable on a young puppy, but will become more evident as the puppy gets older. The puppy you choose should also have an healthy-looking coat, an important indication of good health internally.

Another factor in your selection is gender; do you want a male or a female? While it is recommended to neuter or spay all dogs and bitches kept solely as pets, those intended for the show ring must be kept sexually 'entire.' In the German Spitz, there are no major differences between the two genders other than that dogs should look masculine and bitches feminine.

Something else to consider is whether or not to take out veterinary insurance. Vet's bills can mount up, and you must always be certain that sufficient funds are available to give your dog any veterinary attention that may be needed. Keep in mind, though, that routine vaccinations will not be covered.

SELECTING A BREEDER AND PUPPY

If you are convinced that the German Spitz is the ideal dog for you, it's time to learn about where to find a puppy and what to look for. You should enquire about breeders who enjoy a good reputation in the breed. You are looking for an established breeder with outstanding dog ethics and a strong commitment to the breed. New owners should have as many questions as they have doubts. An established breeder is indeed the one to answer your four million questions and make you comfortable with your choice of the German Spitz. An established breeder will sell you a puppy at a fair price if, and only if, the breeder determines that you are a suitable, worthy owner of his dogs. An established breeder can be relied upon for advice, no matter what time of day or night. A reputable breeder will accept a puppy back, without questions, should you decide that this is not the right dog for you.

When choosing a breeder, reputation is much more

INSURANCE

Many good breeders will offer you insurance with your new puppy, which is an excellent idea. The first few weeks of insurance will probably be covered free of charge or with only minimal cost, allowing you to take up the policy when this expires. If you own a pet dog, it is sensible to take out such a policy as veterinary fees can be high, although routine vaccinations and boosters are not covered. Look carefully at the many options open to you before deciding which suits you best.

PUPPY SELECTION

Your selection of a good puppy can be determined by your needs. A show potential or a good pet? It is your choice. Every puppy, however, should be of good temperament. Although show-quality puppies are bred and raised with emphasis on physical conformation, responsible breeders strive for equally good temperament. Do not buy from a breeder who concentrates solely on physical beauty at the expense of personality.

DOCUMENTATION

Two important documents you will get from the breeder are the pup's pedigree and registration certificate. The breeder should register the litter and each pup with The Kennel Club, and it is necessary for you to have the paperwork if you plan on showing or breeding in the future.

Make sure you know the breeder's intentions on which type of registration he will obtain for the pup. There are limited registrations which may prohibit the dog from being shown, bred or competing in non-conformation trials such as Working or Agility if the breeder feels that the pup is not of sufficient quality to do so. There is also a type of registration that will permit the dog in non-conformation competition only.

On the reverse side of the registration certificate, the new owner can find the transfer section, which must be signed by the breeder.

Watching the breeder interact with her dogs lets you know how she cares for them and, thus, how she raises her puppies.

important than convenience of location.

Choosing a breeder is an important first step in dog ownership. Fortunately, the majority of German Spitz breeders is devoted to the breed and its well-being. The Kennel Club is

BOY OR GIRL?

An important consideration to be discussed is the sex of your puppy. Gender will play a part in your selection of a show or breeding dog, but the pup's individual personality, regardless of sex, is most important when choosing a pet. It is always advisable to neuter or spay a pet, which may guarantee your German Spitz a longer life.

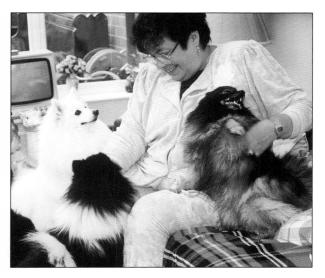

able to recommend reputable breeders of quality German Spitzen, as can any local all-breed club or German Spitz club.

Once you have contacted and met a breeder or two and made your choice about which breeder is best suited to your needs, it's time to visit the litter. Keep in mind that many top breeders have waiting lists. Sometimes new owners have to wait as long as two years for a puppy. If you are really committed to the breeder whom you've selected, then you will wait (and hope for an early arrival!). If not, you may have to resort to your second- or third-choice breeder. Don't be too anxious, however. If the breeder doesn't have a waiting list, or any customers, there is probably a good reason. It's no different than visiting a pub with no clientele. The better pubs and restaurants always have waiting lists—and it's usually worth the wait. Besides, isn't a puppy more important than a pint?

Since you are likely to be choosing a German Spitz as a pet dog and not a show dog, you simply should select a pup that is friendly, attractive and healthy. German Spitzen generally have small litters, with Kleins averaging three puppies and Mittels averaging about five puppies, so selection will be somewhat limited once you have located a desirable litter.

Breeders commonly allow visitors to see their litters by around the fifth or sixth week,

PUPPY APPEARANCE
Your puppy should have a well-fed appearance but not a distended abdomen, which may indicate worms or incorrect feeding, or both. The body should be firm, with a solid feel. The skin of the abdomen should be pale pink and clean, without signs of scratching or rash. Check the hind legs to make certain that dewclaws were removed, if any were present at birth.

DID YOU KNOW?
You should not even think about buying a puppy that looks sick, undernourished, overly frightened or nervous. Sometimes a timid puppy will warm up to you after a 30-minute 'let's-get-acquainted' session.

and puppies leave for their new homes between the eighth and tenth week. Breeders who permit their puppies to leave early are more interested in your pounds than in their puppies' well-being. Puppies need to learn the rules of the pack from their dams, and most dams continue teaching the pups manners and dos and don'ts until around the eighth week. Breeders spend significant amounts of time with the German Spitz toddlers so that the pups are able to interact with the 'other species,' i.e. humans. Given the long history that dogs and humans have, bonding between the two species is natural but must be nurtured. A well-bred, well-socialised German Spitz pup wants nothing more than to be near you and please you.

Watching litter-mates play and interact with their dam and each other is perhaps the best indicator of each pup's individual personality.

INHERIT THE MIND
In order to know whether or not a puppy will fit into your lifestyle, you need to assess his personality. A good way to do this is to interact with his parents. Your pup inherits not only his appearance but also his personality and temperament from the sire and dam. If the parents are fearful or overly aggressive, these same traits may likely show up in your puppy.

COMMITMENT OF OWNERSHIP
After considering all of these factors, you have most likely already made some very important decisions about selecting your puppy. You have chosen a German Spitz, which means that you have decided which characteristics you want in a dog and what type of dog will best fit into your family and lifestyle. If you have selected a breeder, you have gone a step further—you have done your research and found a responsible, conscientious person who breeds quality German Spitzen and who should be a reliable source of help

as you and your puppy adjust to life together. If you have observed a litter in action, you have obtained a firsthand look at the dynamics of a puppy 'pack' and, thus, you have learned about each pup's individual personality—perhaps you have even found one that particularly appeals to you.

However, even if you have not yet found the German Spitz puppy of your dreams, observing pups will help you learn to recognise certain behaviour and to determine what a pup's behaviour indicates about his temperament. You will be able to pick out which pups are the leaders, which ones are less outgoing, which ones are confident, which ones are shy, playful, friendly, aggressive, etc. Equally as important, you will learn to recognise what an healthy pup should look and act like. All of these things will help you in your search, and when you find the German Spitz that was meant for you, you will know it!

Researching your breed, selecting a responsible breeder and observing as many pups as possible are all important steps on the way to dog ownership. It may seem like a lot of effort…and you have not even taken the pup home yet! Remember, though, you cannot be too careful when it comes to deciding on the type of dog you want and finding out about your prospective pup's background. Buying a puppy is not—or should not be—just another whimsical purchase. This is one instance in which you actually do get to choose your own family!

You may be thinking that buying a puppy should be fun—it should not be so serious and so much work. Keep in mind that your puppy is not a cuddly stuffed toy or decorative lawn ornament; rather, he is a living creature that will become a real member of your family. You will come to realise that, while buying a puppy is a pleasurable and exciting endeavour, it is not something to be taken lightly. Relax…the fun will start when the pup comes home!

'YOU BETTER SHOP AROUND!'

Finding a reputable breeder that sells healthy pups is very important, but make sure that the breeder you choose is not only someone you respect but also with whom you feel comfortable. Your breeder will be a resource long after you buy your puppy, and you must be able to call with reasonable questions without being made to feel like a pest! If you don't connect on a personal level, investigate some other breeders before making a final decision.

new home, he will fall into his place in the family quite naturally. However, it never hurts to emphasise the commitment of dog ownership. With some time and patience, it is really not too difficult to raise a curious and exuberant German Spitz pup to be a well-adjusted and well-mannered adult dog—a dog that could be your most loyal friend.

PREPARING PUPPY'S PLACE IN YOUR HOME

Researching your breed and finding a breeder are only two aspects of the 'homework' you will have to do before taking your German Spitz puppy home. You will also have to prepare your home and family for the new addition. Much as you would prepare a nursery for a newborn baby, you will need to designate a place in your home that will be the puppy's own. How you prepare your home will depend

Meet all of the dogs on the breeder's premises, especially the parents of the litter, if possible. The looks and temperaments of the adult dogs give you valuable insight into how puppies of that breeder's line mature.

Always keep in mind that a puppy is nothing more than a baby in a furry disguise…a baby who is virtually helpless in a human world and who trusts his owner for fulfilment of his basic needs for survival. In addition to food, water and shelter, your pup needs care, protection, guidance and love. If you are not prepared to commit to this, then you are not prepared to own a dog.

Wait a minute, you say. How hard could this be? All of my neighbours own dogs and they seem to be doing just fine. Why should I have to worry about all of this? Well, you should not worry about it; in fact, you will probably find that once your German Spitz pup gets used to his

ARE YOU A FIT OWNER?
If the breeder from whom you are buying a puppy asks you a lot of personal questions, do not be insulted. Such a breeder wants to be sure that you will be a fit provider for his puppy.

TIME TO GO HOME

Breeders rarely release puppies until they are eight to ten weeks of age. This is an acceptable age for most breeds of dog, excepting toy breeds, which are not released until around 12 weeks, given their petite sizes. If a breeder has a puppy that is 12 weeks of age or older, it is likely well socialised and house-trained. Be sure that it is otherwise healthy before deciding to take it home.

German Spitz Klein.

A MATTER OF SIZE

Because sizes are not yet completely stabilised between Kleins and Mittels, if size is important to you (for example, for future breeding or for the show ring), this should be made clear to the breeder. It is very wise to look into the sizes of a puppy's parents and to enquire about the sizes of their ancestors.

German Spitz Mittel.

on how much freedom the dog will be allowed. Whatever you decide, you must ensure that he has a place that he can 'call his own.'

When you bring your new puppy into your home, you are bringing him into what will become his home as well. Obviously, you did not buy a puppy with the intentions of catering to his every whim and allowing him to 'rule the roost,' but in order for a puppy to grow into a stable, well-adjusted dog, he has to feel comfortable in his surroundings. Remember, he is leaving the warmth and security of his mother and littermates, as well as the familiarity of the only place he has ever known, so it is important to make his transition as easy as possible. By preparing a place in your home for the puppy, you are making him feel as welcome as possible in a strange

PHOTO COURTESY OF DOSKOCIL

WHAT YOU SHOULD BUY

CRATE

To someone unfamiliar with the use of crates in dog training, it may seem like punishment to shut a dog in a crate, but this is not the case at all. Although all breeders do not advocate crate training, more and more breeders and trainers are recommending crates as preferred tools for show puppies as well as pet puppies.

Crates are not cruel—crates have many humane and highly effective uses in dog care and training. For example, crate training is a popular and very successful house-training method. In addition, a crate can keep your dog safe during travel and, perhaps most importantly, a crate provides your dog with a place of his own in your home. It serves as a 'doggie bedroom' of sorts—your German Spitz can curl up in his crate when he wants to sleep or when he just needs a break. Many dogs sleep in their crates overnight. With soft bedding and his favourite toy, a crate becomes a cosy pseudo-den for your dog. Like his ancestors, he too will seek out the comfort and retreat of a den—you just happen to be providing him with something a little more luxurious than what his early ancestors enjoyed.

As far as purchasing a crate, the type that you buy is up to you. It will most likely be one of the

new place. It should not take him long to get used to it, but the sudden shock of being trans-planted is somewhat traumatic for a young pup. Imagine how a small child would feel in the same situation—that is how your puppy must be feeling. It is up to you to reassure him and to let him know, 'Little chap, you are going to like it here!'

CRATE TRAINING TIPS

During crate training, you should partition off the section of the crate in which the pup stays. If he is given too big an area, this will hinder your training efforts. Crate training is based on the fact that a dog does not like to soil his sleeping quarters, so it is ineffective to keep a pup in a crate that is so big that he can eliminate in one end and get far enough away from it to sleep. Also, you want to make the crate den-like for the pup. Blankets and a favourite toy will make the crate cosy for the small pup; as he grows, you may want to evict some of his 'roommates' to make more room. It will take some coaxing at first, but be patient. Given some time to get used to it, your pup will adapt to his new home-within-a-home quite nicely.

two most popular types: wire or fibreglass. There are advantages and disadvantages to each type. For example, a wire crate is more open, allowing the air to flow through and affording the dog a view of what is going on around him, while a fibreglass crate is sturdier. Both can double as travel crates, providing protection for the dog.

The size of the crate is another thing to consider. It is best to get one that will accommodate your dog both as a pup and at full size. Because of the wide range of sizes in this breed, the crate size required will vary, but there is always a good variety of crates in the smaller sizes available at major dog shows and pet shops. Use eventual size as a guide and purchase a crate in which your German Spitz will be able to stand and lie down comfortably at his projected adult height.

BEDDING

Veterinary bedding in the dog's crate will help the dog feel more at home, and you may also like to pop in a small blanket. First, this will take the place of the leaves, twigs, etc., that the pup would use in the wild to make a den; the

Crates are ideal for various purposes, including house-training, safety and quiet refuge.

TOYS, TOYS, TOYS!

With a big variety of dog toys available, and so many that look like they would be a lot of fun for a dog, be careful in your selection. It is amazing what a set of puppy teeth can do to an innocent-looking toy, so, obviously, safety is a major consideration. Be sure to choose the most durable products that you can find. Hard nylon bones and toys are a safe bet, and many of them are offered in different scents and flavours that will be sure to capture your dog's attention. It is always fun to play a game of catch with your dog, and there are balls and flying discs that are specially made to withstand dog teeth.

pup can make his own 'burrow' in the crate. Although your pup is far removed from his den-making ancestors, the denning instinct is still a part of his genetic makeup. Second, until you take your pup home, he has been sleeping amid the warmth of his mother and littermates, and while a blanket is not the same as a warm, breathing body, it still provides heat and something with which to snuggle. You will want to wash your pup's bedding frequently in case he has a toileting 'accident' in his crate, and replace or remove any blanket that becomes ragged and starts to fall apart.

Toys

Toys are a must for dogs of all ages, especially for curious playful pups. Puppies are the 'children' of the dog world, and what child does not love toys? Chew toys provide enjoyment for both dog and owner—your dog will enjoy playing with his favourite toys, while you will enjoy the fact that they distract him from chewing on your expensive shoes and leather sofa. Puppies love to chew; in fact, chewing is a physical need for pups as they are teething, and everything looks appetising! The full range of your possessions—from old tea towel to Oriental carpet—are fair game in the eyes of a teething pup. Puppies are not all that discerning when it comes to finding something literally to 'sink their teeth into'—everything tastes great!

German Spitz puppies are not particularly aggressive chewers, but they do enjoy chew toys. Only the safe, durable toys, with no removable parts, should be offered to them. Special caution must be taken with stuffed toys, because they can become de-stuffed in no time. The overly excited pup may ingest the stuffing, which is neither digestible nor nutritious. Similarly, squeaky toys are quite popular, but must be checked regularly to see that there is no danger of the 'squeak' becoming loose and being swallowed. Perhaps a squeaky toy can be used as an aid in training, but not for unsupervised play. Monitor the condition of all your pup's toys carefully and get rid of any that have been chewed to the point of becoming potentially dangerous.

Be careful of natural bones, which have a tendency to splinter into sharp, dangerous pieces. Also be careful of rawhide, which can turn into pieces that are easy to swallow and become a mushy mess on your carpet.

LEAD

A nylon lead is probably the best option, as it is the most resistant to puppy teeth should your pup take a liking to chewing on his lead. Of course, this is an habit that should be nipped in the bud, but, if your pup likes to chew on his lead, he has a very slim chance of being able to chew through the strong nylon. Nylon leads are also lightweight, which is good for a young German Spitz who is just getting used to the idea of walking on a lead. For everyday walking and safety purposes, the nylon lead is a good choice.

As your pup grows up and gets used to walking on the lead, you may want to purchase a flexible lead. These leads allow you to extend the length to give the dog a broader area to explore or to shorten the length to keep the dog near you.

Pet shops usually stock a wide assortment of leads. German Spitz require only lightweight nylon leads.

Durable, easily cleaned bowls for food and water are the best choices. German Spitzen do not require large feeding vessels.

PHOTO COURTESY OF MIKKI PET PRODUCTS.

COLLAR

Your pup should get used to wearing a collar all the time since you will want to attach his ID tags to it; plus, you have to attach the lead to something! A lightweight nylon collar is a good choice. Make certain that the collar fits snugly enough so that the pup cannot wriggle out of it, but is loose enough so that it will not be uncomfortably tight around the pup's neck. You should be able to fit a finger between the pup's neck and the collar. It may take some time for your pup to get used to wearing the collar, but soon he will not even notice that it is there.

Choke collars are made for training, but are not appropriate for use with the German Spitz. This is too harsh a method for a small breed, not to mention that it will also damage the German Spitz's long, abundant coat.

FOOD AND WATER BOWLS

Your pup will need two bowls, one for food and one for water. You may want two sets of bowls, one for indoors and one for outdoors, depending on where the dog will be fed and where he will be spending time. Stainless steel or sturdy plastic bowls are popular choices. Plastic bowls are more chewable, but dogs tend not to chew on the steel variety, which can be sterilised. It is important to buy sturdy bowls

CHOOSE AN APPROPRIATE COLLAR

The **BUCKLE COLLAR** is the standard collar used for everyday purposes. Be sure that you adjust the buckle on growing puppies. Check it every day. It can become too tight overnight! These collars can be made of leather or nylon. Attach your dog's identification tags to this collar.

The **CHOKE COLLAR** is constructed of highly polished steel so that it slides easily through the stainless steel loop. The idea is that the dog controls the pressure around its neck and he will stop pulling if the collar becomes uncomfortable. This collar is not recommended for heavily coated dogs like the German Spitz.

The **HALTER** is for a trained dog that has to be restrained to prevent running away, chasing a cat and the like. Considered the most humane of all collars, it is frequently used on smaller dogs for which collars are not comfortable.

find out what else you need as you go along—grooming supplies, flea/tick protection, baby gates to partition a room, etc. These things will vary depending on your situation, but it is important that you have everything you need to feed and make your German Spitz comfortable in his first few days at home.

PUPPY-PROOFING YOUR HOME
Aside from making sure that your German Spitz will be comfortable in your home, you also have to make sure that your home is safe for your dog. This means taking precautions that your pup will not get into anything he should not get into and that there is nothing within his reach that may harm

since anything is in danger of being chewed by puppy teeth and you do not want your dog to be constantly chewing apart his bowl (for his safety and for your purse!).

It is your responsibility to clean up after your German Spitz has relieved himself. Pet shops offer various tools to aid in the cleanup task.

CLEANING SUPPLIES
Until a pup is house-trained, you will be doing a lot of cleaning. 'Accidents' will occur, which is acceptable in the beginning stages of toilet training because the puppy does not know any better. All you can do is be prepared to clean up any accidents as soon as they happen. Old rags, towels, newspapers and a safe disinfectant are good to have on hand.

BEYOND THE BASICS
The items previously discussed are the bare necessities. You will

him should he sniff it, chew it, inspect it, etc. This probably seems obvious since, while you are primarily concerned with your pup's safety, at the same time you do not want your belongings to be ruined. Breakables should be placed out of reach if your dog is to have full run of the house. If he is to be limited to certain places within the house, keep any potentially dangerous items in the 'off-limits' areas.

An electrical cord can pose a danger should the puppy decide to taste it—and who is going to convince a pup that it would not make a great chew toy? Cords should be fastened tightly against the wall. If your dog is going to spend time in a crate, make sure that there is nothing near his crate that he can reach if he sticks his curious little nose or paws through the openings. Just as you would with a child, keep all household cleaners and chemicals where the dog cannot reach them.

It is also important to make sure that the outside of your home is safe. Of course, your puppy should never be unsupervised, but a pup let loose in the garden will want to run and explore, and he should be granted that freedom. Do not let a fence give you a false sense of security; you would be surprised at how crafty (and persistent) a dog can be in working out how to dig under and squeeze his way through small

holes, or to jump or climb over a fence.

The remedy is to make the fence well embedded into the ground and high enough so that it really is impossible for your dog to climb over it. German Spitz are not especially known as climbers, diggers or jumpers, but of course one can always come across the occasional escape artist!

About a four-foot fence should be sufficient for the German Spitz. Be sure to repair or secure any gaps in the fence. Check the fence periodically to ensure that it is in good shape and make repairs as needed; a very determined pup may return to the same spot to 'work on it' until he is able to get through.

FIRST TRIP TO THE VET
You have selected your puppy, and your home and family are ready. Now all you have to do is collect your German Spitz from the breeder and the fun begins,

SKULL & CROSSBONES
Thoroughly puppy-proof your house before bringing your puppy home. Never use cockroach or rodent poisons or plant fertilisers in any area accessible to the puppy. Avoid the use of toilet cleaners. Most dogs are born with 'toilet sonar' and will take a drink if the lid is left open. Also keep the rubbish secured and out of reach.

is not an aggressive breed, even though it is a good watchdog. The males even remain non-aggressive when a bitch is in season. Therefore, your German Spitz should enjoy making acquaintances of all species!

Once your pup has received his necessary vaccinations, feel free to take him out and about (on his lead, of course). Walk him around the neighbourhood, take him on your daily errands, let people pet him, let him meet other dogs and pets, etc. Puppies do not have to try to make friends; there will be no shortage of people who will want to introduce themselves. Just make sure that you carefully supervise each meeting. If the neighbourhood children want to say hello, for example, that is great—children and pups most often make great companions. However, sometimes an excited child can unintentionally handle a pup too roughly, or an overzealous pup can playfully nip a little too hard.

You want to make socialisation experiences positive ones. What a pup learns during this very formative stage will affect his attitude toward future encounters. You want your dog to be comfortable around everyone. A pup that has a bad experience with a child may grow up to be a dog that is shy around or aggressive toward children.

PROPER SOCIALISATION

The socialisation period for puppies is from age 8 to 16 weeks. This is the time when puppies need to leave their birth family and take up residence with their new owners, where they will meet many new people, other pets, etc. Failure to be adequately socialised can cause the dog to grow up fearing others and being shy and unfriendly due to a lack of self-confidence.

CONSISTENCY IN TRAINING

Dogs, being pack animals, naturally need a leader, or else they try to establish dominance in their packs. When you welcome a dog into your family, the choice of who becomes the leader and who

MANNERS MATTER

During the socialisation process, a puppy should meet people, experience different environments and definitely be exposed to other canines. Through playing and interacting with other dogs, your puppy will learn lessons, ranging from controlling the pressure of his jaws by biting his littermates to the inner-workings of the canine pack that he will apply to his human relationships for the rest of his life. That is why removing a puppy from its litter too early (before eight weeks) can be detrimental to the pup's development.

Puppies should be allowed to nurse from their mothers for about the first six weeks, although, starting around the third or fourth week, the breeder will begin to introduce small portions of suitable solid food. Most breeders like to introduce alternate milk and meat meals initially, building up to weaning time.

By the time the puppies are seven or a maximum of eight weeks old, they should be fully weaned and fed solely on a proprietary puppy food. Selection of the most suitable, good-quality diet at this time is essential, for a puppy's fastest growth rate is during the first year of life. Veterinary surgeons are usually able to offer advice in this regard.

The frequency of meals will be reduced over time and eventually you will switch to feeding adult food. The age at which you do this can vary according to the make of food used and to bodily development. German Spitzen generally can be changed to an adult diet by 10 to 12 months of age, but this varies very much according to personal preference and to the brand used. Some brands have a slight variation for 'juniors'; for a small breed, a 'small bite' (smaller pieces) food is a wise choice.

Puppy and junior diets should be well balanced for the needs of your dog so that, except in certain circumstances, additional

vitamins, minerals and proteins will not be required.

ADULT DIETS

A dog is considered an adult when it has stopped growing. Most German Spitzen will reach

CHANGE IN DIET

As your dog's caretaker, you know the importance of keeping his diet consistent, but sometimes when you run out of food or if you're on holiday, you have to make a change quickly. Some dogs will experience digestive problems, but most will not. If you are planning on changing your dog's menu, do so gradually to ensure that your dog will not have any problems. Over a period of four to five days, slowly add some new food to your dog's old food, increasing the percentage of new food each day.

their full height during puppyhood but, as sizes are not yet completely stabilised, it should be appreciated that different lines may mature at different rates. Again, in general the diet of a German Spitz can be changed to an adult one at about 10 to 12 months of age. You should rely upon your veterinary surgeon or dietary specialist to recommend an acceptable mainte-nance diet. Major dog food manufacturers specialise in this type of food, and it is merely necessary for you to select the one best suited to your dog's needs. Active dogs may have different requirements than sedate dogs.

Senior Diets

As dogs get older, their metabo-lism changes. The older dog usually exercises less, moves more slowly and sleeps more. This change in lifestyle and physiological performance requires a change in diet. Since

A good-quality complete adult dog food should provide your German Spitz with all of the necessary nutrients.

FEEDING TIPS

Dog food must be at room tempera-ture, neither too hot nor too cold. Fresh water, changed daily and served in a clean bowl, is mandatory, especially when feeding dried food.

Never feed your dog from the table while you are eating, and never feed your dog leftovers from your own meal. They usually contain too much fat and too much seasoning.

Dogs must chew their food. Hard pellets are excellent; soups and slurries are to be avoided.

Don't add leftovers or "people food" to normal dog food. The normal food is usually balanced, and adding something extra destroys the balance.

Except for age-related changes, dogs do not require dietary variations. They can be fed the same diet, day after day, without becoming ill.

these changes take place slowly, they might not be recognisable. What is easily recognisable is weight gain. By continuing to feed your dog an adult-maintenance diet when it is slowing down metabolically, your dog will gain weight. Obesity in an older dog compounds the health problems that already accompany old age.

As your dog gets older, few of his organs function up to par. The kidneys slow down and the intestines become less efficient. These age-related factors are best handled with a change in diet and

A Worthy Investment

Veterinary studies have proven that a balanced high-quality diet pays off in your dog's overall health, coat quality, behaviour and activity level. Invest in premium brands for the maximum payoff with your dog.

a change in feeding schedule to give smaller portions that are more easily digested. There is no single best diet for every older dog. While many dogs do well on light or senior diets, other dogs do better on puppy diets or other special premium diets such as lamb and rice. Some German Spitzen are switched to senior food at around seven or eight years of age, while others never change. Be sensitive to your senior German Spitz's diet, as this will help control other problems that may arise with your old friend.

WATER

Just as your dog needs proper nutrition from his food, water is an essential 'nutrient' as well. Water keeps the dog's body properly hydrated and promotes normal function of the body's systems. During house-training, it is necessary to keep an eye on how much water your German Spitz is drinking, but once he is

A group of thirsty German Spitzen, gathering 'round the water bowl.

GRAIN-BASED DIETS

Some less expensive dog foods are based on grains and other plant proteins. While these products may appear to be attractively priced, many breeders prefer a diet based on animal proteins and believe that they are more conducive to your dog's health. Many grain-based diets rely on soy protein, which may cause flatulence (passing gas).

There are many cases, however, when your dog might require a special diet. These special requirements should only be recommended by your veterinary surgeon.

reliably trained he should have access to clean fresh water at all times, especially if you feed dried food. Make certain that the dog's water bowl is clean, and change the water often.

EXERCISE

Although the German Spitz is a small breed, it is a very active one, so exercise is necessary for both its health and happiness. Although the breed can usually cope with more exercise than might be anticipated for its size, German Spitzen don't actually need to be exercised for miles each day. However, they do appreciate an opportunity to explore new surroundings and smells.

Exercising your German Spitz can be enjoyable and healthy for both of you. Brisk walks, once the puppy reaches three or four months of age, will stimulate heart rates and build muscle for both dog and owner. As the dog reaches adulthood, the speed and distance of the walks can be increased as long as they are both kept reasonable and comfortable for both of you. Keep in mind that German Spitzen should not be allowed to jump strenuously, particularly not down from high places. Exercise up and down

Playtime with his owner is a good source of exercise for the energetic German Spitz, as well as a wonderful opportunity for dog and owner to spend time together.

'DOES THIS COLLAR MAKE ME LOOK FAT?'

While humans may obsess about how they look and how trim their bodies are, many people believe that extra weight on their dogs is a good thing. The truth is, pets should not be over- or under-weight, as both can lead to or signal sickness. In order to tell how fit your pet is, run your hands over his ribs. Are his ribs buried under a layer of fat or are they sticking out consider-ably? If your pet is within his normal weight range, you should be able to feel the ribs easily, but they should not protrude abnormally. If you stand above him, the outline of his body should resemble an hourglass, although with the German Spitz's abundant coat, looks can be deceiving. Making sure your dog is the right weight for his breed will certainly contribute to his good health.

stairs should be restricted, or at least supervised.

Play sessions in the garden and letting the dog run free in the garden under your supervision also are sufficient forms of

EXERCISE ALERT!

You should be careful where you exercise your dog. Many countryside areas have been sprayed with chemicals that are highly toxic to both dogs and humans. Never allow your dog to eat grass or drink from puddles on either public or private grounds, as the run-off water may contain chemicals from sprays and herbicides.

DRINK, DRANK, DRUNK— MAKE IT A DOUBLE

In both humans and dogs, as well as most other living organisms, water forms the major part of nearly every body tissue. Naturally, we take water for granted, but without it, life as we know it would cease.

For dogs, water is needed to keep their bodies functioning biochemically. Additionally, water is needed to replace the water lost while panting. Unlike humans, who are able to sweat to dissipate heat, dogs must pant to cool down, thereby losing the vital water from their bodies needed to regulate their body temperatures. Humans lose electrolyte-containing products and other body-fluid components through sweating; dogs do not lose anything except water.

Water is essential always, but especially so when the weather is hot or humid or when your dog is exercising or working vigorously.

TIPPING THE SCALES

Good nutrition is vital to your dog's health, but many people end up over-feeding or giving unnecessary supplements. Here are some common doggie diet don'ts:
- Adding milk, yoghurt and cheese to your dog's diet may seem like a good idea for coat and skin care, but dairy products are very fattening and can cause indigestion.
- Diets high in fat will not cause heart attacks in dogs but will certainly cause your dog to gain weight.
- Most importantly, don't assume your dog will simply stop eating once he doesn't need any more food. Given the chance, he will eat you out of house and home!

exercise for the German Spitz. Fetching games can be played indoors or out; these are excellent for giving your dog active play that he will enjoy. Chasing things that move comes naturally to dogs of all breeds. When your German Spitz runs after the ball or object, praise him for picking it up and encourage him to bring it back to you for another throw. Never go to the object and pick it up yourself, or you'll soon find that you are the one retrieving the objects rather than the dog! If you choose to play games outdoors, you must have a securely fenced-in garden and/or have the dog attached to at least an 8-metre (26-foot) light line for security. You want your German Spitz to run, but not run away!

When allowing a dog to run free, safety is of utmost importance. For this reason, all possible escape routes should be thoroughly checked out before letting a dog off the lead and, of course, your garden must be safely enclosed by fencing, which should be checked at regular intervals.

Bear in mind that an overweight dog should never be suddenly over-exercised; instead he should be encouraged to increase exercise slowly. Not only is exercise essential to keep the dog's body fit, it is essential to his mental well-being. A bored dog will find something to do, which often manifests itself in some type of destructive behaviour. In this sense, exercise is essential for the owner's mental well-being as well!

GROOMING

Because of his double coat, your German Spitz will need to be groomed regularly. Thus, it is essential that short grooming sessions be introduced from a very early age. From the very beginning, a few minutes each day should be set aside so that your puppy becomes familiar with the process. Set aside a grooming area, ideally a special grooming table with a non-slip surface. In

this way, your puppy will learn to associate that place with his grooming sessions and, of course, to behave. If your puppy is taught to behave well for these sessions, grooming will be a pleasure both for the dog and for you.

German Spitzen do not actually need as much grooming as some of the longer-coated breeds, but nonetheless the coat does need work and an owner needs to be dedicated to keeping the coat in tip-top condition. Daily grooming is not usually necessary, but a quick brushing every other day is advisable, with a thorough grooming session on a weekly basis. Owners must be aware that the coat will change considerably as the puppy matures into adulthood, and there

Grooming the German Spitz's glorious double coat is a responsibility to which every owner must commit.

Your local pet shop will have a selection of grooming tools from which you can choose what you need to keep your German Spitz's coat in top condition.

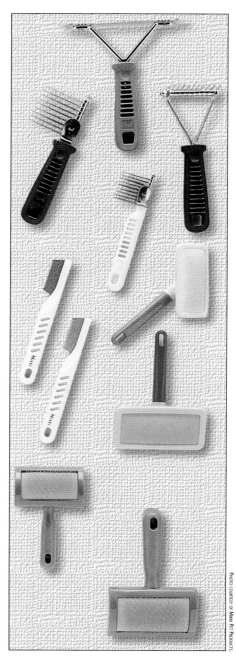

GROOMING EQUIPMENT

How much grooming equipment you purchase will depend on how much grooming you are going to do. Here are some basics:

- Grooming table
- Bristle or pin brush
- Soft brush
- Wide-toothed comb
- Scissors
- Rubber mat
- Dog shampoo
- Spray hose attachment
- Towels
- Blaster
- Ear cleaner
- Cotton wipes
- Nail clippers

may be some shedding around spring and autumn. Hormonal changes can play havoc with a coat, so be prepared for this around the time of a bitch's season.

ROUTINE COAT MAINTENANCE

To keep your German Spitz looking in tip-top condition, it is important to keep the coat clean and to groom regularly. Many owners bath their dogs only infrequently, providing that plenty of attention is paid to grooming sessions. It should always be borne in mind that dirt and dust, if allowed to accumulate, are both drying and abrasive

on him and you have made sure that he cannot escape from the garden or wriggle out of his collar and run away from you. However, accidents can happen and there may come a time when your dog unexpectedly becomes separated from you. If this unfortunate event should occur, the first thing on your mind will be finding him. Proper identification, including an ID tag, a tattoo and possibly a microchip, will increase the chances of his being returned to you safely and quickly.

IDENTIFICATION OPTIONS

As puppies become more and more expensive, especially those puppies of high quality for showing and/or breeding, they have a greater chance of being stolen. The usual collar dog tag is, of course, easily removed. But there are two more permanent techniques that have become widely used for identification.

The puppy microchip implantation involves the injection of a small microchip, about the size of a corn kernel, under the skin of the dog. If your dog shows up at a clinic or shelter, or is offered for resale under less-than-savoury circumstances, it can be positively identified by the microchip. The microchip is scanned, and a registry quickly identifies you as the owner. This is not only protection against theft, but should the dog run away or go chasing a squirrel and become lost, you have a fair chance of his being returned to you.

Tattooing is done on various parts of the dog, from his belly to his cheeks. The number tattooed can be your telephone number or any other number that you can easily memorise. When professional dog thieves see a tattooed dog, they usually lose interest. Both microchipping and tattooing can be done at your local veterinary clinic. For the safety of our dogs, no laboratory facility or dog broker will accept a tattooed dog as stock.

Living with an untrained dog is a lot like owning a piano that you do not know how to play—it is a nice object to look at but it does not do much more than that to bring you pleasure. Now try taking piano lessons, and suddenly the piano comes alive and brings forth magical sounds and rhythms that set your heart singing and your body swaying.

The same is true with your German Spitz. Any dog is a big responsibility and, if not trained sensibly, may develop unacceptable behaviour that annoys you or could even cause family friction.

To train your German Spitz, you may like to enrol in an obedience class. Teach your dog good manners as you learn how and why he behaves the way he does. Find out how to communicate with your dog and how to recognise and understand his communications with you. Suddenly the dog takes on a new role in your life—he is clever, interesting, well behaved and fun to be with. He demonstrates his bond of devotion to you daily. In other words, your German Spitz does wonders for your ego because he constantly reminds you that you are not only his leader, you are his hero!

Those involved with teaching dog obedience and counselling

PARENTAL GUIDANCE

Training a dog is a life experience. Many parents admit that much of what they know about raising children they learned from caring for their dogs. Dogs respond to love, fairness and guidance, just as children do. Become a good dog owner and you may become an even better parent.

owners about their dogs' behaviour have discovered some interesting facts about dog ownership. For example, training dogs when they are puppies results in the highest rate of success in developing well-mannered and well-adjusted adult dogs. Training an older dog, from six months to six years of age, can produce almost equal results, providing that the owner accepts the dog's slower rate of learning capability and is willing to work patiently to help the dog succeed at developing to his fullest potential. Unfortunately, many owners of untrained adult dogs lack the patience factor, so they do not persist until their dogs are successful at learning particular behaviours.

Training a puppy aged 10 to 16 weeks (20 weeks at the most) is like working with a dry sponge in a pool of water. The pup soaks up whatever you show him and

Training includes not only teaching the basic commands and house-training but also teaching the rules of the house and good manners—such as not begging at the table.

THE HAND THAT FEEDS

To a dog's way of thinking, your hands are like his mouth in terms of a defence mechanism. If you squeeze him too tightly, he might just bite you because that would be his normal response. This is not aggressive biting and, although all biting should be discouraged, you need the discipline in learning how to handle your dog.

constantly looks for more things to do and learn. At this early age, his body is not yet producing hormones, and therein lies the reason for such an high rate of success. Without hormones, he is focused on his owners and not particularly interested in investigating other places, dogs, people, etc. You are his leader: his provider of food, water, shelter and security. He latches onto you and wants to stay close. He will usually follow you from room to room, will not let you out of his sight when you are outdoors with him and will respond in like manner to the people and animals you encounter. If you greet a friend warmly, he will be happy to greet the person as well. If, however, you are hesitant or anxious about the approach of a stranger, he will respond accordingly.

Once the puppy begins to produce hormones, his natural curiosity emerges and he begins to

Puppies tend to follow their owners, but curiosity often gets the best of them. Don't be surprised if something else catches your small spitz's attention and he's off in another direction.

REAP THE REWARDS

If you start with a normal, healthy dog and give him time, patience and some carefully executed lessons, you will reap the rewards of that training for the life of the dog. And what a life it will be! The two of you will find immeasurable pleasure in the companionship you have built together with love, respect and understanding.

investigate the world around him. It is at this time when you may notice that the untrained dog begins to wander away from you and even ignore your commands to stay close. When this behaviour becomes a problem, you have two choices: get rid of the dog or train him. It is strongly urged that you choose the latter option.

You usually will be able to find obedience classes within a reasonable distance from your home, but you can also do a lot to train your dog yourself. Sometimes there are classes available, but the tuition is too costly. Whatever the circumstances, the solution to training your dog without obedience classes lies within the pages of this book.

This chapter is devoted to helping you train your German Spitz at home. If the recommended procedures are followed faithfully, you may expect positive results that will prove rewarding both to you and your dog.

Whether your new charge is a puppy or a mature adult, the methods of teaching and the techniques we use in training basic behaviours are the same. After all, no dog, whether puppy or adult, likes harsh or inhumane methods. All creatures, however, respond favourably to gentle motivational methods and sincere praise and encouragement. Now let us get started.

HOUSE-TRAINING

You can train a puppy to relieve himself wherever you choose, but this must be somewhere suitable. You should bear in mind from the outset that when your puppy is old enough to go out in public places, any canine deposits must be removed at once. You will always have to carry with you a small plastic bag or 'poop-scoop.'

Outdoor training includes such surfaces as grass, soil and cement. Indoor training usually means training your dog to newspaper. When deciding on the surface and location that you will want your German Spitz to use, be sure it is going to be permanent. Training your dog to grass and then changing your mind a few months later is extremely difficult for both dog and owner.

Next, choose the command you will use each and every time you want your puppy to void.

TRAINING TIP
Dogs will do anything for your attention. If you reward the dog when he is calm and attentive, you will develop a well-mannered dog. If, on the other hand, you greet your dog excitedly and encourage him to wrestle with you, the dog will greet you the same way and you will have a hyperactive dog on your hands.

'Hurry up' and 'Toilet' are two examples of commands that are commonly used by dog owners. Get in the habit of giving the puppy your chosen relief command before you take him out. That way, when he becomes an adult, you will be able to determine if he wants to go out when you ask him. A confirmation will be signs of interest, wagging his tail, watching you intently, going to the door, etc.

PUPPY'S NEEDS

Puppy needs to relieve himself after play periods, after each meal, after he has been sleeping and at any time he indicates that he is looking for a place to urinate or defecate. The urinary and intestinal tract muscles of very young puppies are not fully developed. Therefore, like human

Breeders often introduce young pups to crates; it will be a great help in house-training if your puppy has already been acclimated to a crate.

babies, puppies need to relieve themselves frequently.

Take your puppy out often—every hour for an eight-week-old, for example—and always immediately after sleeping and eating. The older the puppy, the less often he will need to relieve himself. Finally, as a mature healthy adult, he will require only three to five relief trips per day.

HOUSING

Since the types of housing and control you provide for your puppy have a direct relationship on the success of house-training, we consider the various aspects of both before we begin training.

Taking a new puppy home and turning him loose in your house can be compared to turning a child loose in a sports arena and telling the child that the place is all his! The sheer enormity of the place would be too much for him to handle. Instead, offer the puppy clearly defined areas where he can play, sleep, eat and live. A

CANINE DEVELOPMENT SCHEDULE

It is important to understand how and at what age a puppy develops into adulthood.
If you are a puppy owner, consult the following Canine Development Schedule to
determine the stage of development your puppy is currently experiencing.
This knowledge will help you as you work with the puppy in the weeks and months ahead.

Period	Age	Characteristics
FIRST TO THIRD	BIRTH TO SEVEN WEEKS	Puppy needs food, sleep and warmth, and responds to simple and gentle touching. Needs mother for security and disciplining. Needs littermates for learning and interacting with other dogs. Pup learns to function within a pack and learns pack order of dominance. Begin socialising with adults and children for short periods. Begins to become aware of its environment.
FOURTH	EIGHT TO TWELVE WEEKS	Brain is fully developed. Needs socialising with outside world. Remove from mother and littermates. Needs to change from canine pack to human pack. Human dominance necessary. Fear period occurs between 8 and 12 weeks. Avoid fright and pain.
FIFTH	THIRTEEN TO SIXTEEN WEEKS	Training and formal obedience should begin. Less association with other dogs, more with people, places, situations. Period will pass easily if you remember this is pup's change-to-adolescence time. Be firm and fair. Flight instinct prominent. Permissiveness and over-disciplining can do permanent damage. Praise for good behaviour.
JUVENILE	FOUR TO EIGHT MONTHS	Another fear period about 7 to 8 months of age. It passes quickly, but be cautious of fright and pain. Sexual maturity reached. Dominant traits established. Dog should understand sit, down, come and stay by now.

NOTE: THESE ARE APPROXIMATE TIME FRAMES. ALLOW FOR INDIVIDUAL DIFFERENCES IN PUPPIES.

room of the house where the family gathers is the most obvious choice. Puppies are social animals and need to feel a part of the pack right from the start. Hearing your voice, watching you while you are doing things and smelling you nearby are all positive reinforcers that he is now a member of your pack. Usually a family room, the kitchen or a nearby adjoining breakfast area is ideal for providing safety and security for both puppy and owner.

Within the designated room, there should be a smaller area that the puppy can call his own. An alcove, a wire or fibreglass dog crate or a fenced (not boarded!) corner from which he can view the activities of his new family will be fine. The size of the area or crate is the key factor here. The area must be large enough so that the puppy can lie down and stretch out, as well as stand up, without rubbing his head on the top. At the same time, it must be small enough so that he cannot relieve himself at one end and sleep at the other without coming into contact with his droppings before he is fully

trained to relieve himself outside. Dogs are, by nature, clean animals and will not remain close to their relief areas unless forced to do so. In those cases, they then become dirty dogs and usually remain that way for life.

The dog's designated area should contain clean bedding and a toy. Water must always be available, in a non-spill container once house-training has been achieved reliably.

CONTROL

By control, we mean helping the puppy to create a lifestyle pattern that will be compatible to that of his human pack (YOU!). Just as we guide little children to learn

HONOUR AND OBEY

Dogs are the most honourable animals in existence. They consider another species (humans) as their own. They interface with you. You are their leader. Puppies perceive children to be on their level; their actions around small children are different from their behaviour around their adult masters.

our way of life, we must show the puppy when it is time to play, eat, sleep, exercise and even entertain himself.

Your puppy should always sleep in his crate. He should also learn that, during times of household confusion and excessive human activity, such as at breakfast when family members are preparing for the day, he can play by himself in relative safety and comfort in his designated area. Each time you leave the puppy alone, he should understand exactly where he is to stay.

Puppies are chewers. They cannot tell the difference between lamp cords, television wires, shoes, table legs, etc. Chewing into a television wire, for example, can be fatal to the puppy, while a shorted wire can start a fire in the house. If the puppy chews on the arm of the chair when he is alone, you will probably discipline him angrily when you get home. Thus, he makes the association that your coming home means he is going to be punished. (He will not remember chewing the chair and is incapable of making the associ-ation of the discipline with his naughty deed.) Accustoming the pup to his designated area not only keeps him safe but also avoids his engaging in destructive behaviours when you are not around.

Always clean up after your German Spitz, whether you are in a public place or in your own garden.

Times of excitement, such as special occasions, family parties, etc., can be fun for the puppy, providing that he can view the activities from the security of his designated area. He is not under-foot and he is not being fed all sorts of titbits that will probably cause him stomach distress, yet he still feels a part of the fun.

SCHEDULE

A puppy should be taken to his relief area each time he is released from his designated area, after meals, after a play session and when he first awakens in the morning (at age eight weeks, this can mean 5 a.m.!). The puppy will indicate that he's ready 'to go' by circling or sniffing busily—do not misinterpret these signs. For a puppy less than ten weeks of age, a routine of taking him out every hour is necessary. As the puppy grows, he will be able to wait for longer periods of time.

Keep trips to his relief area short. Stay no more than five or six minutes and then return to the house. If he goes during that time, praise him lavishly and take him indoors immediately. If he does not, but he has an accident when you go back indoors, pick him up immediately, say 'No! No!' and return to his relief area. Wait a few minutes, then return to the house again. Never hit a puppy or rub his face in urine or excrement when he has had an accident!

Once indoors, put the puppy in his crate until you have had time to clean up his accident. Then, release him to the family area and watch him more closely than before. Chances are, his accident was a result of your not picking up his signal or waiting too long before offering him the opportunity to relieve himself. Never hold a grudge against the puppy for accidents.

HOW MANY TIMES A DAY?

AGE	RELIEF TRIPS
To 14 weeks	10
14–22 weeks	8
22–32 weeks	6
Adulthood (dog stops growing)	4

These are estimates, of course, but they are a guide to the MINIMUM opportunities a dog should have each day to relieve itself.

Let the puppy learn that going outdoors means it is time to relieve himself, not to play. Once trained, he will be able to play indoors and out and still differentiate between the times for play versus the times for relief.

Help him develop regular hours for naps, being alone, playing by himself and just resting, all in his crate. Encourage him to entertain himself while you are busy with your activities. Let him learn that having you near is comforting, but it is not

one of the primary ingredients in house-training your puppy is control. Regardless of your lifestyle, there will always be occasions when you will need to have a place where your dog can stay and be happy and safe. Crate training is the answer for now and in the future.

In conclusion, a few key elements are really all you need for a successful house-training method—consistency, frequency, praise, control and supervision. By following these procedures with a normal, healthy puppy, you and the puppy will soon be past the stage of 'accidents' and ready to move on to a full and rewarding life together.

your main purpose in life to provide him with undivided attention.

Each time you put your puppy in his own area, use the same command, whatever suits best. Soon he will run to his crate or special area when he hears you say those words.

Crate training provides safety for you, the puppy and the home. It also provides the puppy with a feeling of security, and that helps the puppy achieve self-confidence and clean habits. Remember that

ROLES OF DISCIPLINE, REWARD AND PUNISHMENT
Discipline, training one to act in accordance with rules, brings order to life. It is as simple as

THE SUCCESS METHOD
6 Steps to Successful Crate Training

1 Tell the puppy 'Crate time!' and place him in the crate with a small treat (a piece of cheese or half of a biscuit). Let him stay in the crate for five minutes while you are in the same room. Then release him and praise lavishly. Never release him when he is fussing. Wait until he is quiet before you let him out.

2 Repeat Step 1 several times a day.

3 The next day, place the puppy in the crate as before. Let him stay there for ten minutes. Do this several times.

4 Continue building time in five-minute increments until the puppy stays in his crate for 30 minutes with you in the room. Always take him to his relief area after prolonged periods in his crate.

5 Now go back to Step 1 and let the puppy stay in his crate for five minutes, this time while you are out of the room.

6 Once again, build crate time in five-minute increments with you out of the room. When the puppy will stay willingly in his crate (he may even fall asleep!) for 30 minutes with you out of the room, he will be ready to stay in it for several hours at a time.

that. Without discipline, particularly in a group society, chaos will reign supreme and the group will eventually perish. Humans and canines are social animals and need some form of discipline in order to function effectively. They must procure food, protect their home base and their young and reproduce to keep their species going. If there were no discipline in the lives of social animals, they would eventually die from starvation and/or predation by other stronger animals.

In the case of domestic canines, discipline in their lives is needed in order for them to understand how their pack (you and other family members) functions and how they must act in order to survive.

A large humane society in an highly populated area recently surveyed dog owners regarding their satisfaction with their relationships with their dogs. People who had trained their dogs were 75% more satisfied with their pets than those who had never trained their dogs.

Dr Edward Thorndike, a psychologist, established *Thorndike's Theory of Learning*, which states that a behaviour that results in a pleasant event tends to be repeated. A behaviour that results in an unpleasant event tends not to be repeated. It is this theory upon which training methods are based today. For example, if you manipulate a dog to perform a specific behaviour and reward him for doing it, he is likely to do it again because he enjoyed the end result.

Occasionally, punishment, a penalty inflicted for an offence, is necessary. The best type of punishment often comes from an outside source. For example, a child is told not to touch the stove because he may get burned. He disobeys and touches the stove. In doing so, he receives a burn. From that time on, he respects the heat of the stove and avoids contact with it. Therefore, a behaviour that results in an unpleasant event tends not to be repeated.

A good example of a dog's

learning the hard way is the dog who chases the house cat. He is told many times to leave the cat alone, yet he persists in teasing the cat. Then, one day, the dog begins chasing the cat but the cat

COMMAND STANCE
Stand up straight and authoritatively when giving your dog commands. Do not issue commands when lying on the floor or lying on your back on the sofa. If you are on your hands and knees when you give a command, your dog will think you are positioning yourself to play.

turns and swipes a claw across the dog's face, leaving the dog with a painful gash on his nose. The final result is that the dog stops chasing the cat. Again, a behaviour that results in an unpleasant event tends not to be repeated.

TRAINING EQUIPMENT

COLLAR AND LEAD
For a German Spitz, the collar and lead that you use for training must be one with which you are easily able to work, not too heavy for the dog and perfectly safe.

TREATS
Have a bag of treats on hand; something nutritious and easy to swallow works best. Use a soft treat, a chunk of cheese or a piece of cooked chicken rather than a

dry biscuit. By the time the dog has finished chewing a dry treat, he will forget why he is being rewarded in the first place!

Using food rewards will not teach a dog to beg at the table—the only way to teach a dog to beg at the table is to give him food from the table. In training, rewarding the dog with a food treat will help him associate praise and the treats with learning new behaviours that obviously please his owner.

TRAINING BEGINS: ASK THE DOG A QUESTION
In order to teach your dog anything, you must first get his attention. After all, he cannot learn anything if he is looking away from you with his mind on something else.

To get your dog's attention, ask him 'School?' and immediately walk over to him and give him a treat as you tell him 'Good dog.' Wait a minute or two and repeat the routine, this time with a treat in your hand as you approach within a foot of the dog. Do not go directly to him, but stop about a foot short of him and hold out the treat as you ask 'School?' He will see you approaching with a treat in your hand and most likely begin walking toward you. As you meet, give him the treat and praise again.

The third time, ask the question, have a treat in your

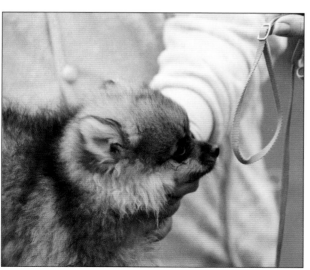

A German Spitz only requires a light nylon collar and lead. The first step in training is accustoming the dog to both.

hand and walk only a short distance toward the dog so that he must walk almost all the way to you. As he reaches you, give him the treat and praise again.

By this time, the dog will probably be getting the idea that if he pays attention to you, especially when you ask that question, it will pay off in treats and enjoyable activities for him. In other words, he learns that 'school' means doing great things with you that are fun and that result in positive attention for him.

Remember that the dog does not understand your verbal language; he only recognises sounds. Your question translates to a series of sounds for him, and those sounds become the signal to go to you and pay attention. The dog learns that if he does this, he will get to interact with you plus receive treats and praise.

THE BASIC COMMANDS

TEACHING SIT

Now that you have the dog's attention, attach his lead and hold it in your left hand, and hold a food treat in your right hand. Place your food hand at the dog's nose and let him lick the treat but not take it from you. Say 'Sit' and slowly raise your food hand from in front of the dog's nose up over his head so that he is looking at the ceiling. As he bends his head

Light pressure on the dog's rear will help guide him into the sit position as you are first teaching the command.

upward, he will have to bend his knees to maintain his balance. As he bends his knees, he will assume a sit position. At that point, release the food treat and praise lavishly with comments such as 'Good dog! Good sit!,' etc. Remember to always praise enthusiastically, because dogs relish verbal praise from their owners and feel so proud of themselves whenever they accomplish a behaviour.

You will not use food forever in getting the dog to obey your commands. Food is only used to teach new behaviours and, once the dog knows what you want when you give a specific command, you will wean him off

DOUBLE JEOPARDY

A dog in jeopardy never lies down. He stays alert on his feet because instinct tells him that he may have to run away or fight for his survival. Therefore, if a dog feels threatened or anxious, he will not lie down. Consequently, it is important to have the dog calm and relaxed as he learns the down exercise.

the food treats but still maintain the verbal praise. After all, you will always have your voice with you, and there will be many times when you have no food rewards but expect the dog to obey.

TEACHING DOWN

Teaching the down exercise is easy when you understand how the dog perceives the down position, and it is very difficult when you do not. Dogs perceive the down position as a submissive one; therefore, teaching the down exercise by using a forceful method can sometimes make the

dog develop such a fear of the down that he either runs away when you say 'Down' or he attempts to snap at the person who tries to force him down.

Have the dog sit close alongside your left leg, facing in the same direction as you are. Hold the lead in your left hand and a food treat in your right. Now place your left hand lightly on the top of the dog's shoulders where they meet above the spinal cord. Do not push down on the dog's shoulders; simply rest your left hand there so you can guide the dog to lie down close to your left leg rather than to swing away from your side when he drops.

Now place the food hand at the dog's nose, say 'Down' very softly (almost a whisper), and slowly lower the food hand to the dog's front feet. When the food hand reaches the floor, begin moving it forward along the floor in front of the dog. Keep talking softly to the dog, saying things like, 'Do you want this treat? You can do this, good dog.' Your reassuring tone of voice will help calm the dog as he tries to follow the food hand in order to get the treat.

When the dog's elbows touch the floor, release the food and praise softly. Try to get the dog to maintain that down position for several seconds before you let him sit up again. The goal here is to get the dog to settle down and not feel threatened in the down position.

TEACHING STAY

It is easy to teach the dog to stay in either a sit or a down position. Again, we use food and praise during the teaching process as we help the dog to understand exactly what it is that we are expecting him to do.

To teach the sit/stay, start with the dog sitting on your left side as before and hold the lead in your left hand. Have a food treat in your right hand and place your food hand at the dog's nose. Say 'Stay' and step out on your right foot to stand directly in front of the dog, toe to toe, as he licks and nibbles the treat. Be sure to keep his head facing upward to maintain the sit position. Count to five and then swing around to stand next to the dog again with him on your left. As soon as you get back to the original position, release the food and praise lavishly.

To teach the down/stay, do the down as previously described. As soon as the dog lies down, say 'Stay' and step out on your right foot just as you did in the sit/stay. Count to five and then return to stand beside the dog with him on your left side. Release the treat and praise as always.

Within a week or ten days, you can begin to add a bit of distance between you and your dog when you leave him. When you do, use your left hand open with the palm facing the dog as a stay signal, much the same as the hand signal a constable uses to stop traffic at a junction. Hold the food treat in your right hand as before, but this time the food will not be touching the dog's nose. He will watch the food hand and quickly learn that he is going to get that treat as soon as you return to his side.

When you can stand 1 metre away from your dog for 30 seconds, you can then begin building time and distance in both stays. Eventually, the dog can be expected to remain in the stay position for prolonged periods of time until you return to

Once the sit has been learned, you can progress to the sit/stay. Note the trainer's hand signal, which acts as a 'stop' sign for the dog.

'WHERE ARE YOU?'

When calling the dog, do not say 'Come.' Say things like, 'Rover, where are you? See if you can find me! I have a biscuit for you!' Keep up a constant line of chatter with coaxing sounds and frequent questions such as, 'Where are you?' The dog will learn to follow the sound of your voice to locate you and receive his reward.

him or call him to you. Always praise lavishly when he stays.

TEACHING COME

If you make teaching 'come' an exciting experience, you should never have a 'student' that does not love the game or that fails to come when called. The secret, it seems, is never to teach the word 'come.'

At times when an owner most wants his dog to come when called, the owner is likely to be upset or anxious and he allows these feelings to come through in the tone of his voice when he calls his dog. Hearing that desperation in his owner's voice, the dog fears the results of going to him and therefore either disobeys outright or runs in the opposite direction. The secret, therefore, is to teach the dog a game and, when you want him to come to you, simply play the game. It is practically a no-fail solution!

To begin, have several members of your family take a few food treats and each go into a different room in the house. Everyone takes turns calling the dog, and each person should celebrate the dog's finding him with a treat and lots of happy praise. When a person calls the dog, he is actually inviting the dog to find him and to get a treat as a reward for 'winning.'

A few turns of the 'Where are you?' game and the dog will understand that everyone is playing the game and that each person has a big celebration awaiting the dog's success at locating him or her. Once the dog learns to love the game, simply calling out 'Where are you?' will bring him running from wherever he is when he hears that all-important question.

The come command is recognised as one of the most important things to teach a dog, but there are trainers who work with thousands of dogs and never

'COME' . . . BACK

Never call your dog to come to you for a correction or scold him when he reaches you. That is the quickest way to turn a 'Come' command into 'Go away fast!' Dogs think only in the present tense, and your dog will connect the scolding with coming to you, not with the misbehaviour of a few moments earlier.

teach the actual word 'come.' Yet these dogs will race to respond to a person who uses the dog's name followed by 'Where are you?' For example, a woman has a 12-year-old companion dog who went blind, but who never fails to locate her owner when asked, 'Where are you?'

Children, in particular, love to play this game with their dogs. Children can hide in smaller places like a shower or bath, behind a bed or under a table. The dog needs to work a little bit harder to find these hiding places, but, when he does, he loves to celebrate with a treat and a tussle with a favourite youngster.

TEACHING HEEL

Heeling means that the dog walks beside the owner without pulling. It takes time and patience on the owner's part to succeed at teaching the dog that he (the owner) will not proceed unless the dog is walking calmly beside him.

Neither pulling out ahead on the lead nor lagging behind is acceptable.

Begin by holding the lead in your left hand as the dog sits beside your left leg. Move the loop end of the lead to your right hand, but keep your left hand short on the lead so that it keeps the dog in close next to you.

Say 'Heel' and step forward on your left foot. Keep the dog close to you and take three steps. Stop and have the dog sit next to you in what we now call the 'heel position.' Praise verbally, but do

Always greet your dog happily and reward him with praise and petting when he comes to you when called.

TUG OF WALK?

If you begin teaching the heel by taking long walks and letting the dog pull you along, he misinterprets this action as an acceptable form of taking a walk. When you pull back on the lead to counteract his pulling, he reads that tug as a signal to pull even harder!

Your goal here is to have the dog walk those three steps without pulling on the lead. Once he will walk calmly beside you for three steps without pulling, increase the number of steps you take to five. When he will walk politely beside you while you take five steps, you can increase the length of your walk to ten steps. Keep increasing the length of your stroll until the dog will

Heeling means that the dog walks politely at your side; keep practising until the dog keeps pace with you...not the other way around.

not touch the dog. Hesitate a moment and begin again with 'Heel,' taking three steps and stopping, at which point the dog is told to sit again.

FEAR AGGRESSION

Pups who are subjected to physical abuse during training commonly end up with behavioural problems as adults. One common result of abuse is fear aggression, in which a dog will lash out, bare his teeth, snarl and finally bite someone by whom he feels threatened. For example, your daughter may be playing with the dog one afternoon. As they play hide-and-seek, she backs the dog into a corner and, as she attempts to tease him playfully, he bites her hand. Examine the cause of this behaviour. Did your daughter ever hit the dog? Did someone who resembles your daughter hit or scream at the dog?

Fortunately, fear aggression is relatively easy to correct. Have your daughter engage in only positive activities with the dog, such as feeding, petting and walking. She should not give any corrections or negative feedback. If the dog still growls or cowers away from her, allow someone else to accompany them. After approximately one week, the dog should feel that he can rely on her for many positive things, and he will also be prevented from reacting fearfully towards anyone who might resemble her.

walk quietly beside you without pulling as long as you want him to heel. When you stop heeling, indicate to the dog that the exercise is over by verbally praising as you pet him and say 'OK, good dog.' The 'OK' is used as a release word, meaning that the exercise is finished and the dog is free to relax.

If you are dealing with a dog who insists on pulling you around, simply 'put on your brakes' and stand your ground until the dog realises that the two of you are not going anywhere until he is beside you and moving at your pace, not his. It may take some time just standing there to convince the dog that you are the leader and that you will be the one to decide on the direction and speed of your travel.

Each time the dog looks up at you or slows down to give a slack lead between the two of you, quietly praise him and say, 'Good heel. Good dog.' Eventually, the dog will begin to respond and within a few days he will be walking politely beside you without pulling on the lead. At first, the training sessions should be kept short and very positive; soon the dog will be able to walk nicely with you for increasingly longer distances. Remember also to give the dog free time and the opportunity to run and play when you have finished heel practice.

WEANING OFF TREATS IN TRAINING

Food treats are used in training new behaviours. Once the dog understands what behaviour goes

HEELING WELL

Teach your dog to HEEL in an enclosed area. Once you think the dog will obey reliably and you want to attempt advanced obedience exercises such as off-lead heeling, test him in a fenced-in area so he cannot run away.

with a specific command, it is time to start weaning him off the food treats. At first, give a treat after each exercise. Then, start to give a treat only after every other exercise. Mix up the times when you offer a food reward and the times when you offer only praise so that the dog will never know when he is going to receive both food and praise and when he is going to receive only praise. This is called a variable ratio reward system. It proves successful because there is always the chance that the owner will produce a treat, so the dog never stops trying for that reward. No matter what, *always* give verbal praise.

OBEDIENCE CLASSES

It is a good idea to enrol in an obedience class if one is available in your area. If yours is a show dog, ringcraft classes would be more appropriate. Many areas have dog clubs that offer basic obedience training as well as preparatory classes for obedience competition. There are also local dog trainers who offer similar classes.

At obedience shows, dogs can earn titles at various levels of competition. The beginning levels of obedience competition include basic behaviours such as sit, down, heel, etc. The more advanced levels of competition include jumping, retrieving, scent

SAFETY FIRST

While it may seem that the most important things to your dog are eating, sleeping and chewing the upholstery on your furniture, his first concern is actually safety. The domesticated dogs we keep as companions have the same pack instinct as their ancestors who ran free thousands of years ago. Because of this pack instinct, your dog wants to know that he and his pack (family) are not in danger of being harmed, and that his pack has a strong, capable leader. You must establish yourself as the leader early on in your relationship. That way your dog will trust that you will take care of him and the pack, and he will accept your commands without question.

discrimination and signal work. The advanced levels require a dog and owner to put a lot of time and effort into their training. The titles that can be earned at these levels of competition are very prestigious.

OTHER ACTIVITIES FOR LIFE

Whether a dog is trained in the structured environment of a class or alone with his owner at home, there are many activities that can bring fun and rewards to both owner and dog once they have mastered basic control. Teaching the dog to help out around the home, in the garden or on the farm provides great satisfaction to both dog and owner. In addition, the dog's help makes life a little easier for his owner and raises his stature as a valued companion to his family. It helps give the dog a purpose by occupying his mind and providing an outlet for his energy.

Backpacking is an exciting and healthy activity that the dog can be taught without assistance from more than his owner. The exercise of walking and climbing is good for man and dog alike, and the bond that they develop together is priceless. The rule for backpacking with any dog is never to expect the dog to carry more than one-sixth of his body weight.

If you are interested in partici-pating in organised competition with your German Spitz, there are activities other than obedience in which you and your dog can become involved. Agility is a popular sport in which dogs run through obstacle courses that

The relationship between an owner and her well-trained dogs is a wonderful one, whether competing, spending quiet time together or just playing around.

include various jumps, tunnels and other exercises to test the dogs' speed and coordination. The German Spitz enjoys agility; it is a sport well-suited to an energetic breed with such a sense of fun.

Mini-agility has been devised by The Kennel Club for small breeds. The events are essentially the same, except all obstacles have been reduced in size so that small dogs can participate. The owners run beside their dogs to give commands and to guide them through the course. Although competitive, the focus is on fun— it's fun to do, fun to watch and great exercise.

FETCH!

Play fetch games with your puppy in an enclosed area where he can retrieve his toy and bring it back to you. Always use a toy or object designated just for this purpose. Never use a shoe, stocking or other item he may later confuse with those in your wardrobe or underneath your chair.

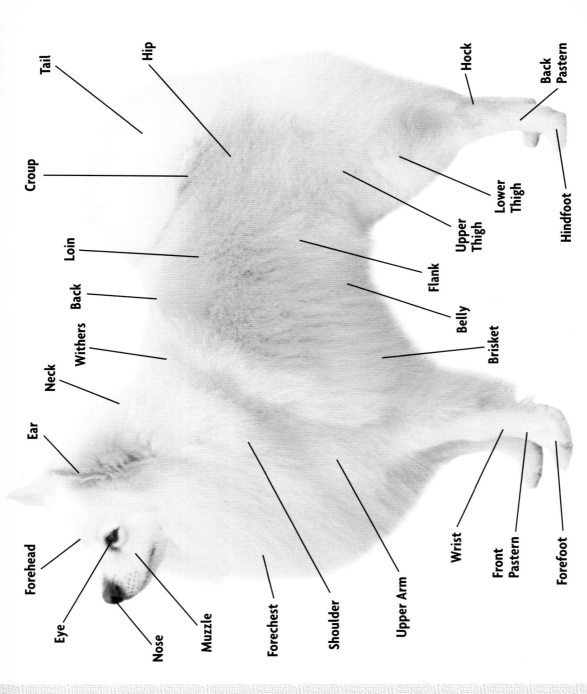

PHYSICAL STRUCTURE OF THE GERMAN SPITZ

immunizing doses of several different viruses such as distemper, parvovirus, parainfluenza and hepatitis, although some veterinary surgeons recommend separate vaccines for each disease. There are other vaccines available when the puppy is at risk. You should rely upon professional advice. This is especially true for the booster-shot programme. Most vaccination programmes require a booster when the puppy is a year old and once a year thereafter. In some cases, circumstances may require more or less frequent immunizations. Kennel cough, more formally known as tracheobron-chitis, is treated with a vaccine that is sprayed into the dog's nostrils. Kennel cough is usually included in routine vaccination, but this is often not so effective as for other major diseases.

WEANING TO FIVE MONTHS OLD
Puppies should be weaned by the time they are about two months old. A puppy that remains for at least eight weeks with its mother and littermates usually adapts better to other dogs and people later in life. Some new owners have their puppies examined by veterinary surgeons immediately, which is a good idea. Vaccination programmes usually begin when

HEALTH AND VACCINATION SCHEDULE

AGE IN WEEKS:	6TH	8TH	10TH	12TH	14TH	16TH	20-24TH	52ND
Worm Control	✔	✔	✔	✔	✔	✔	✔	
Neutering								✔
Heartworm		✔		✔		✔	✔	
Parvovirus	✔		✔		✔		✔	✔
Distemper		✔		✔		✔		✔
Hepatitis		✔		✔		✔		✔
Leptospirosis								✔
Parainfluenza	✔		✔		✔			✔
Dental Examination		✔					✔	✔
Complete Physical		✔					✔	✔
Coronavirus				✔			✔	✔
Kennel Cough	✔							
Hip Dysplasia								✔
Rabies							✔	

Vaccinations are not instantly effective. It takes about two weeks for the dog's immune system to develop antibodies. Most vaccinations require annual booster shots. Your veterinary surgeon should guide you in this regard.

  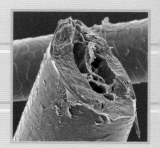

Normal hairs of a dog enlarged 200 times original size. The cuticle (outer covering) is clean and healthy. Unlike human hair that grows from the base, a dog's hair also grows from the end. Damaged hairs and split ends, illustrated above.

SCANNING ELECTRON MICROGRAPHS BY DR DENNIS KUNKEL, UNIVERSITY OF HAWAII

DISEASE REFERENCE CHART

	What is it?	What causes it?	Symptoms
Leptospirosis	Severe disease that affects the internal organs; can be spread to people.	A bacterium, which is often carried by rodents, that enters through mucous membranes and spreads quickly throughout the body.	Range from fever, vomiting and loss of appetite in less severe cases to shock, irreversible kidney damage and possibly death in most severe cases.
Rabies	Potentially deadly virus that infects warm-blooded mammals. Not seen in United Kingdom.	Bite from a carrier of the virus, mainly wild animals.	1st stage: dog exhibits change in behaviour, fear. 2nd stage: dog's behaviour becomes more aggressive. 3rd stage: loss of coordination, trouble with bodily functions.
Parvovirus	Highly contagious virus, potentially deadly.	Ingestion of the virus, which is usually spread through the faeces of infected dogs.	Most common: severe diarrhoea. Also vomiting, fatigue, lack of appetite.
Kennel cough	Contagious respiratory infection.	Combination of types of bacteria and virus. Most common: *Bordetella bronchiseptica* bacteria and parainfluenza virus.	Chronic cough.
Distemper	Disease primarily affecting respiratory and nervous system.	Virus that is related to the human measles virus.	Mild symptoms such as fever, lack of appetite and mucous secretion progress to evidence of brain damage, 'hard pad.'
Hepatitis	Virus primarily affecting the liver.	Canine adenovirus type I (CAV-1). Enters system when dog breathes in particles.	Lesser symptoms include listlessness, diarrhoea, vomiting. More severe symptoms include 'blue-eye' (clumps of virus in eye).
Coronavirus	Virus resulting in digestive problems.	Virus is spread through infected dog's faeces.	Stomach upset evidenced by lack of appetite, vomiting, diarrhoea.

the puppy is very young.

The puppy will have its teeth examined, and have its skeletal conformation and general health checked prior to certification by the veterinary surgeon. Puppies in certain breeds may have problems with their kneecaps, cataracts and other eye problems, heart murmurs or undescended testicles. They may also have personality problems, and your veterinary surgeon might have training in temperament evaluation.

FIVE TO TWELVE MONTHS OF AGE
Unless you intend to breed or show your dog, neutering the puppy at six months of age is recommended. Discuss this with your veterinary surgeon. Neutering (for males) and spaying (for females) has proven to be extremely beneficial. Besides eliminating the possibility of pregnancy, it inhibits (but does not prevent) breast cancer in bitches and prostate cancer in male dogs. Under no circumstances should a bitch be spayed prior to her first season.

Your veterinary surgeon should provide your puppy with a thorough dental evaluation at six months of age, ascertaining whether all of the permanent teeth have erupted properly. An home dental-care regimen should be initiated at six months, including brushing weekly and providing good dental devices (such as nylon bones). Regular dental care promotes healthy teeth, fresh breath and a longer life.

OLDER THAN ONE YEAR

Once a year, your grown dog should visit the vet for an examination and vaccination boosters, if needed. Some vets recommend blood tests, a thyroid level check and a dental evaluation to accompany these annual visits. A thorough clinical evaluation by the vet can provide critical background information for your dog. Blood tests are often performed at one year of age, and dental examinations around the third or fourth birthday. In the long run, quality preventative care for your pet can save money, teeth and lives.

SKIN PROBLEMS

Veterinary surgeons are consulted by dog owners for skin problems more than for any other group of diseases or maladies. Dogs' skin is almost as sensitive as human skin, and both suffer from almost the same ailments (though the occurrence of acne in dogs is rare!). For this reason, veterinary dermatology has developed into a speciality practised by many veterinary surgeons.

Dogs of any breed can sometimes suffer skin problems, which can take the form of alopaecia, displayed by a loss of hair. In such cases, a lamb and rice diet, coupled with additional vitamin E intake, can be beneficial; of course, you should always check with your vet. Hypothyroidism is another very serious problem that can affect coat growth. This, too, can occur in many breeds, so should be investigated and not dismissed until checked.

Since many skin problems have visual symptoms that are almost identical, it requires the skill of an experienced veterinary dermatologist to identify and cure many of the more severe skin disorders. Pet shops sell many treatments for skin problems, but most of the treatments are

KNOW WHEN TO POSTPONE A VACCINATION

While the visit to the vet is costly, it is never advisable to update a vaccination when visiting with a sick or pregnant dog. Vaccinations should be avoided for all elderly dogs. If your dog is showing the signs of any illness or any medical condition, no matter how serious or mild, including skin irritations, do not vaccinate. Likewise, a lame dog should never be vaccinated; any dog undergoing surgery or on any immunosuppressant drugs should not be vaccinated until fully recovered.

DO YOU KNOW ABOUT HIP DYSPLASIA?

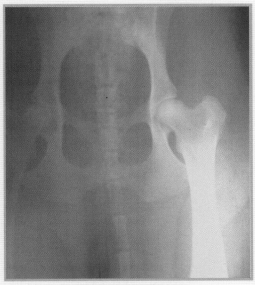

X-ray of a dog with 'Good' hips.

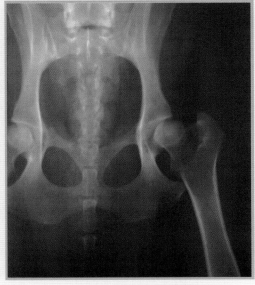

X-ray of a dog with 'Moderate' dysplastic hips.

Hip dysplasia is a fairly common condition found in pure-bred dogs. When a dog has hip dysplasia, its hind leg has an incorrectly formed hip joint. By constant use of the hip joint, it becomes more and more loose, wears abnormally and may become arthritic.

Hip dysplasia can only be confirmed with an x-ray, but certain symptoms may indicate a problem. Your dog may have a hip dysplasia problem if it walks in a peculiar manner, hops instead of smoothly runs, uses its hind legs in unison (to keep the pressure off the weak joint), has trouble getting up from a prone position or always sits with both legs together on one side of its body.

As the dog matures, it may adapt well to life with a bad hip, but in a few years the arthritis develops and many dogs with hip dysplasia become cripples.

Hip dysplasia is considered an inherited disease and only can be diagnosed definitively when the dog is two years old. Some experts claim that a special diet might help your puppy outgrow the bad hip, but the usual treatments are surgical. The removal of the pectineus muscle, the removal of the round part of the femur, reconstructing the pelvis and replacing the hip with an artificial one are all surgical interventions that are expensive, but they are usually very successful. Follow the advice of your veterinary surgeon.

directed at the symptoms and not the underlying problem(s). If your dog is suffering from a skin disorder, you should seek professional assistance as quickly as possible. As with all diseases, the earlier a problem is identified and treated, the more successful is the cure.

HEREDITARY SKIN DISORDERS

Veterinary dermatologists are currently researching a number of skin disorders that are believed to have an hereditary basis. These inherited diseases are transmitted by both parents, who appear (phenotypically) normal but have a recessive gene for the disease, meaning that they carry, but are not affected by, the disease. These diseases pose serious problems to breeders because in some instances there are no methods of identifying carriers. Often the secondary diseases associated with these skin conditions are even more debilitating than the skin disorders themselves, including cancers and respiratory problems.

Among the hereditary skin disorders, for which the mode of inheritance is known, are acrodermatitis, cutaneous asthenia (Ehlers-Danlos syndrome), sebaceous adenitis, cyclic hematopoiesis, dermatomyositis, IgA deficiency, colour dilution alopaecia and nodular dermatofibrosis. Some of these disorders are limited to one or two breeds,

BE CAREFUL WHERE YOU WALK YOUR DOG
Dogs who have been exposed to lawns sprayed with herbicides have double and triple the rate of malignant lymphoma. Town dogs are especially at risk, as they are exposed to tailored lawns and gardens. Dogs perspire and absorb through their footpads. Be careful where your dog walks and always avoid any area that appears yellowed from chemical overspray. These chemicals are not good for you, either!

while others affect a large number of breeds. All inherited diseases must be diagnosed and treated by a veterinary specialist.

PARASITE BITES

Many of us are allergic to insect bites. The bites itch, erupt and may even become infected. Dogs have the same reaction to fleas, ticks and/or mites. When an insect lands on you, you have the chance to whisk it away with your hand. Unfortunately, when your dog is bitten by a flea, tick or mite, he can only scratch it away or bite it. By the time the dog has been bitten, the parasite has done some of its damage. It may also have laid eggs, which will cause further problems in the near future. The itching from parasite bites is probably due to the saliva

the dog. Traditionally, this would be in the form of a collar or a spray, but more recent innovations include digestible insecticides that poison the fleas when they ingest the dog's blood. Alternatively, there are drops that, when placed on the back of the animal's neck, spread throughout the fur and skin to kill adult fleas.

DID YOU KNOW?

Never mix flea control products without first consulting your vet. Some products can become toxic when combined with others and can cause fatal consequences.

INSECT GROWTH REGULATOR (IGR)

Two types of products should be used when treating fleas—a product to treat the pet and a product to treat the home. Adult fleas represent less than 1% of the flea population. The pre-adult fleas (eggs, larvae and pupae) represent more than 99% of the flea population and are found in the environment; it is in the case of pre-adult fleas that products containing an Insect Growth Regulator (IGR) should be used in the home.

IGRs are a new class of compounds used to prevent the development of insects. They do not kill the insect outright, but instead use the insect's biology against it to stop it from completing its growth. Products that contain methoprene are the world's first and leading IGRs. Used to control fleas and other insects, this type of IGR will stop flea larvae from developing and protect the house for up to seven months.

TICKS AND MITES

Though not as common as fleas, ticks and mites are found all over the tropical and temperate world. They don't bite, like fleas; they harpoon. They dig their sharp proboscis (nose) into the dog's skin and drink the blood. Their only food and drink is dog's blood. Dogs can get Lyme disease, Rocky Mountain spotted fever (normally found in the US only), paralysis and many other diseases from ticks and mites. They may live where fleas are found and they like to hide in cracks or seams in walls wherever dogs live. They are controlled the same way fleas are controlled.

The dog tick, *Dermacentor variabilis*, may well be the most common dog tick in many geographical areas, especially those areas where the climate is hot and humid. Most dog ticks

A brown dog tick, *Rhipicephalus sanguineus*, is an uncommon but annoying tick found on dogs.
PHOTO BY CAROLINA BIOLOGICAL SUPPLY/PHOTOTAKE

The head of a dog tick, *Dermacentor variabilis*, enlarged and colorized for effect.

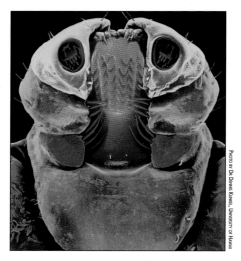

PHOTO BY DR DENNIS KUNKEL, UNIVERSITY OF HAWAII

DEER TICK CROSSING

The great outdoors may be fun for your dog, but it also is an home to dangerous ticks. Deer ticks carry a bacterium known as *Borrelia burgdorferi* and are most active in the autumn and spring. When infections are caught early, penicillin and tetracycline are effective antibiotics, but if left untreated the bacteria may cause neurological, kidney and cardiac problems as well as long-term trouble with walking and painful joints.

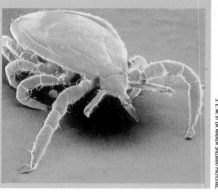

S. E. M. BY DR ANDREW SPIELMAN/PHOTOTAKE.

have life expectancies of a week to six months, depending upon climatic conditions. They can neither jump nor fly, but they can crawl slowly and can range up to 5 metres (16 feet) to reach a sleeping or unsuspecting dog.

Human lice look like dog lice; the two are closely related.

PHOTO BY DWIGHT R KUHN

MANGE

Mites cause a skin irritation called mange. Some mites are contagious, like *Cheyletiella*, ear mites, scabies and chiggers. Mites that cause ear-mite infestations are usually controlled with

Lindane, which can only be administered by a vet, followed by Tresaderm at home. It is essential that your dog be treated for mange as quickly as possible because some forms of mange are transmissible to people.

Opposite page:
The dog tick, *Dermacentor variabilis*, is probably the most common tick found on dogs. Look at the strength in its eight legs! No wonder it's hard to detach them.

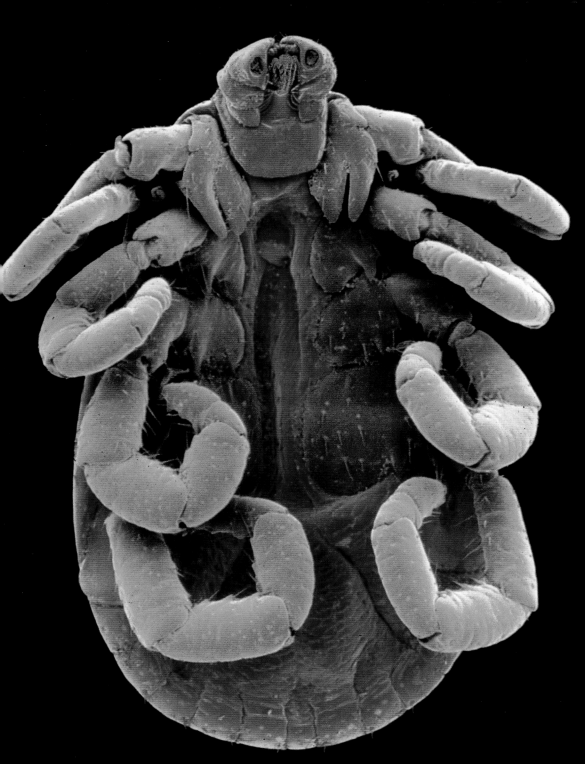

The mange mite,
Psoroptes bovis.

INTERNAL PARASITES

Most animals—fishes, birds and
mammals, including dogs and
humans—have worms and other
parasites that live inside their
bodies. According to Dr Herbert R
Axelrod, the fish pathologist,
there are two kinds of parasites:
dumb and smart. The smart
parasites live in peaceful coopera-
tion with their hosts (symbiosis),
while the dumb parasites kill
their hosts. Most of the worm
infections are relatively easy to
control. If they are not controlled,
they weaken the host dog to the
point that other medical problems

occur, but they do not kill the
host as dumb parasites would.

ROUNDWORMS

The roundworms that infect dogs
are known scientifically as
Toxocara canis. They live in the
dog's intestines. The worms shed
eggs continually. It has been
estimated that a dog produces
about 150 grammes of faeces
every day. Each gramme of faeces
averages 10,000–12,000 eggs of
roundworms. There are no known
areas in which dogs roam that do
not contain roundworm eggs. The
greatest danger of roundworms is

ROUNDWORMS

Average-size dogs can pass 1,360,000 roundworm eggs every day. For example, if there were only 1 million dogs in the world, the world would be saturated with 1,300 metric tonnes of dog faeces. These faeces would contain 15,000,000,000 roundworm eggs.

Up to 31% of home gardens and children's play boxes in the US contain roundworm eggs.

Flushing dog's faeces down the toilet is not a safe practice because the usual sewage treatments do not destroy roundworm eggs.

Infected puppies start shedding roundworm eggs at 3 weeks of age. They can be infected by their mother's milk.

that they infect people too! It is wise to have your dog tested regularly for roundworms.

Pigs also have roundworm infections that can be passed to humans and dogs. The typical roundworm parasite is called *Ascaris lumbricoides.*

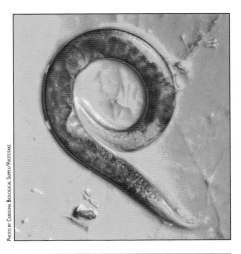

PHOTO BY CAROLINA BIOLOGICAL SUPPLY/PHOTOTAKE

The roundworm *Rhabditis* can infect both dogs and humans.

DEWORMING

Ridding your puppy of worms is *very important* because certain worms that puppies carry, such as tapeworms and roundworms, can infect humans.

Breeders initiate deworming programmes at or about four weeks of age. The routine is repeated every two or three weeks until the puppy is three months old. The breeder from whom you obtained your puppy should provide you with the complete details of the deworming programme.

Your veterinary surgeon can prescribe and monitor the programme of deworming for you. The usual programme is treating the puppy every 15–20 days until the puppy is positively worm-free. It is advised that you only treat your puppy with drugs that are recommended professionally.

The common roundworm, *Ascaris lumbricoides.*

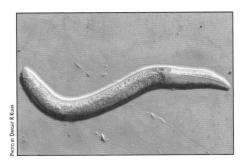

PHOTO BY DWIGHT R. KUHN

Left: *Ancylostoma caninum* are uncommonly found in pet or show dogs in Britain.

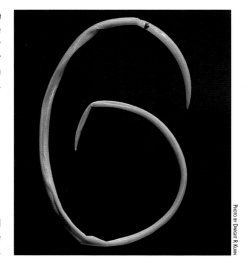

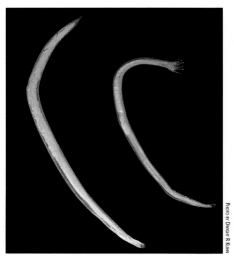

Right: Male and female hookworms.

HOOKWORMS

The worm *Ancylostoma caninum* is commonly called the dog hookworm. It is also dangerous to humans and cats. It has teeth by which it attaches itself to the intestines of the dog. It changes the site of its attachment about six times a day and the dog loses blood from each detachment, possibly causing iron-deficiency anaemia. Hookworms are easily purged from the dog with many medications. Milbemycin oxime, which also serves as an heartworm preventative in

The infective stage of the hookworm larva.

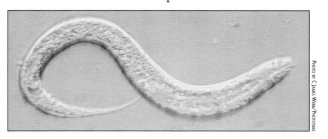

Collies, can be used for this purpose.

In Britain the 'temperate climate' hookworm (*Uncinaria stenocephala*) is rarely found in pet or show dogs, but can occur in hunting packs, racing Greyhounds and sheepdogs because the worms can be prevalent wherever dogs are exercised regularly on grassland.

TAPEWORMS

There are many species of tapeworm, all of which are carried by fleas! The dog eats the flea and starts the tapeworm cycle. Humans can also be infected with tapeworms—so don't eat fleas! Fleas are so small that your dog could pass them onto your hands, your plate or your food and thus make it possible for you to ingest a flea that is carrying tapeworm eggs.

PHOTO BY DWIGHT R KUHN

PHOTO BY DWIGHT R KUHN

PHOTO BY C JAMES WEBB/PHOTOTAKE

TAPEWORMS

Humans, rats, squirrels, foxes, coyotes, wolves and domestic dogs are all susceptible to tapeworm infection. Except in humans, tapeworms are usually not a fatal infection. Infected individuals can harbour 1000 parasitic worms.

Tapeworms, like some other types of worm, are hermaphroditic, meaning male and female in the same worm.

If dogs eat infected rats or mice, they get the tapeworm disease. One month after attaching to a dog's intestine, the worm starts shedding eggs. These eggs are infective immediately. Infective eggs can live for a few months without an host animal.

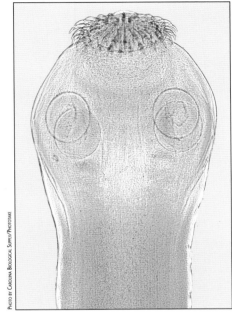

PHOTO BY CAROLINA BIOLOGICAL SUPPLY/PHOTOTAKE

The head and rostellum (the round prominence on the scolex) of a tapeworm, which infects dogs and humans.

While tapeworm infection is not life-threatening in dogs (smart parasite!), it can be the cause of a very serious liver disease for humans. About 50 percent of the humans infected with *Echinococcus multilocularis*, a type of tapeworm that causes alveolar hydatis, perish.

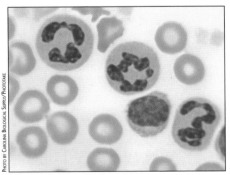

PHOTO BY CAROLINA BIOLOGICAL SUPPLY/PHOTOTAKE

Magnified heartworm larvae, *Dirofilaria immitis.*

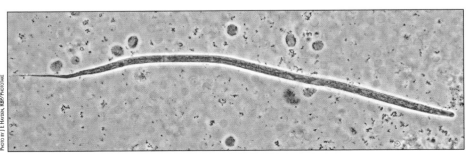

PHOTO BY J E HAYDEN, RBP/PHOTOTAKE

Heartworm, *Dirofilaria immitis.*

First Aid at a Glance

Burns
Place the affected area under cool water; use ice if only a small area is burnt.

Insect bites
Apply ice to relieve swelling; antihistamine dosed properly.

Animal bites
Clean any bleeding area; apply pressure until bleeding subsides; go to the vet.

Spider bites
Use cold compress and a pressurised pack to inhibit venom's spreading.

Antifreeze poisoning
Induce vomiting with hydrogen peroxide. Seek *immediate* veterinary help!

Fish hooks
Removal best handled by vet; hook must be cut in order to remove.

Snake bites
Pack ice around bite; contact vet quickly; identify snake for proper antivenin.

Car accident
Move dog from roadway with blanket; seek veterinary aid.

Shock
Calm the dog, keep him warm; seek immediate veterinary help.

Nosebleed
Apply cold compress to the nose; apply pressure to any visible abrasion.

Bleeding
Apply pressure above the area; treat wound by applying a cotton pack.

Heat stroke
Submerge dog in cold bath; cool down with fresh air and water; go to the vet.

Frostbite/Hypothermia
Warm the dog with a warm bath, electric blankets or hot water bottles.

Abrasions
Clean the wound and wash out thoroughly with fresh water; apply antiseptic.

 Remember: an injured dog may attempt to bite an helping hand from fear and confusion. Always muzzle the dog before trying to offer assistance.

HEARTWORMS

Heartworms are thin, extended worms up to 30 cms (12 ins) long, which live in a dog's heart and the major blood vessels surrounding it. Dogs may have up to 200 worms. Symptoms may be loss of energy, loss of appetite, coughing, the development of a pot belly and anaemia.

Heartworms are transmitted by mosquitoes. The mosquito drinks the blood of an infected dog and takes in larvae with the blood. The larvae, called microfilaria, develop within the body of the mosquito and are passed on to the next dog bitten after the larvae mature. It takes two to three weeks for the larvae to develop to the infective stage within the body of the mosquito. Dogs should be treated at about six weeks of age, and maintained on a prophylactic dose given monthly.

Blood testing for heartworms is not necessarily indicative of how seriously your dog is infected. This is a dangerous disease. Although heartworm is a problem for dogs in America, Australia, Asia and Central Europe, dogs in the United Kingdom are not currently affected by heartworm.

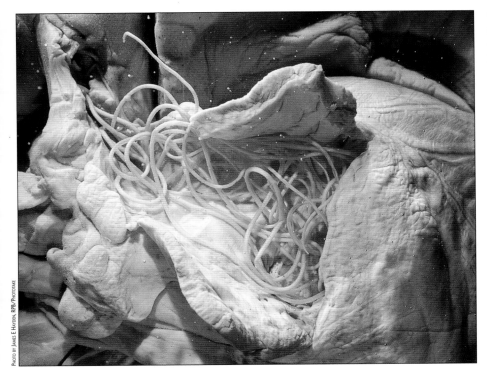

The heart of a dog infected with canine heartworm, *Dirofilaria immitis.*

HOMEOPATHY:
an alternative to conventional medicine

'Less is Most'

Using this principle, the strength of an homeopathic remedy is measured by the number of serial dilutions that were undertaken to create it. The greater the number of serial dilutions, the greater the strength of the homeopathic remedy. The potency of a remedy that has been made by making a dilution of 1 part in 100 parts (or 1/100) is 1c or 1cH. If this remedy is subjected to a series of further dilutions, each one being 1/100, a more dilute and stronger remedy is produced. If the remedy is diluted in this way six times, it is called 6c or 6cH. A dilution of 6c is 1 part in 1,000,000,000,000. In general, higher potencies in more frequent doses are better for acute symptoms and lower potencies in more infrequent doses are more useful for chronic, long-standing problems.

CURING OUR DOGS NATURALLY

Holistic medicine means treating the whole animal as a unique, perfect living being. Generally, holistic treatments do not suppress the symptoms that the body naturally produces, as do most medications prescribed by conventional doctors and vets. Holistic methods seek to cure disease by regaining balance and harmony in the patient's environment. Some of these methods include use of nutritional therapy, herbs, flower essences, aromatherapy, acupuncture, massage, chiropractic and, of course, the most popular holistic approach, homeopathy.

Homeopathy is a theory or system of treating illness with small doses of substances which, if administered in larger quantities, would produce the symptoms that the patient already has. This approach is often described as 'like cures like.' Although modern veterinary medicine is geared toward the 'quick fix,' homeopathy relies on the belief that, given the time, the body is able to heal itself and return to its natural, healthy state.

Choosing a remedy to cure a problem in our dogs is the difficult part of homeopathy. Consult with your veterinary surgeon for a professional diagnosis of your dog's symptoms. Often these symptoms require immediate conventional care. If your vet is willing, and knowledgeable, you may attempt an homeopathic remedy. Be aware that cortisone prevents homeopathic remedies from working. There are hundreds of possibilities and combinations to cure many problems in dogs, from basic physical problems such as excessive moulting, fleas or other parasites, unattractive doggy odour, bad breath, upset tummy, obesity,

dry, oily or dull coat, diarrhoea, ear problems or eye discharge (including tears and dry or mucousy matter), to behavioural abnormalities such as fear of loud noises, habitual licking, poor appetite, excessive barking and various phobias. From alumina to zincum metallicum, the remedies span the planet and the imagination…from flowers and weeds to chemicals, insect droppings, diesel smoke and volcanic ash.

Using 'Like to Treat Like'

Unlike conventional medicines that suppress symptoms, homeopathic remedies treat illnesses with small doses of substances that, if administered in larger quantities, would produce the symptoms that the patient already has. While the same homeopathic remedy can be used to treat different symptoms in different dogs, here are some interesting remedies and their uses.

Apis Mellifica
(made from honey bee venom) can be used for allergies or to reduce swelling that occurs in acutely infected kidneys.

Diesel Smoke
can be used to help control travel sickness.

Calcarea Fluorica
(made from calcium fluoride, which helps harden bone structure) can be useful in treating hard lumps in tissues.

Natrum Muriaticum
(made from common salt, sodium chloride) is useful in treating thin, thirsty dogs.

Nitricum Acidum
(made from nitric acid) is used for symptoms you would expect to see from contact with acids, such as lesions, especially where the skin joins the linings of body orifices or openings such as the lips and nostrils.

Symphytum
(made from the herb Knitbone, *Symphytum officianale*) is used to encourage bones to heal.

Urtica Urens
(made from the common stinging nettle) is used in treating painful, irritating rashes.

HOMEOPATHIC REMEDIES FOR YOUR DOG

Symptom/Ailment	Possible Remedy
ALLERGIES	Apis Mellifica 30c, Astacus Fluviatilis 6c, Pulsatilla 30c, Urtica Urens 6c
ALOPAECIA	Alumina 30c, Lycopodium 30c, Sepia 30c, Thallium 6c
ANAL GLANDS (BLOCKED)	Hepar Sulphuris Calcareum 30c, Sanicula 6c, Silicea 6c
ARTHRITIS	Rhus Toxicodendron 6c, Bryonia Alba 6c
CATARACT	Calcarea Carbonica 6c, Conium Maculatum 6c, Phosphorus 30c, Silicea 30c
CONSTIPATION	Alumina 6c, Carbo Vegetabilis 30c, Graphites 6c, Nitricum Acidum 30c, Silicea 6c
COUGHING	Aconitum Napellus 6c, Belladonna 30c, Hyoscyamus Niger 30c, Phosphorus 30c
DIARRHOEA	Arsenicum Album 30c, Aconitum Napellus 6c, Chamomilla 30c, Mercurius Corrosivus 30c
DRY EYE	Zincum Metallicum 30c
EAR PROBLEMS	Aconitum Napellus 30c, Belladonna 30c, Hepar Sulphuris 30c, Tellurium 30c, Psorinum 200c
EYE PROBLEMS	Borax 6c, Aconitum Napellus 30c, Graphites 6c, Staphysagria 6c, Thuja Occidentalis 30c
GLAUCOMA	Aconitum Napellus 30c, Apis Mellifica 6c, Phosphorus 30c
HEAT STROKE	Belladonna 30c, Gelsemium Sempervirens 30c, Sulphur 30c
HICCOUGHS	Cinchona Deficinalis 6c
HIP DYSPLASIA	Colocynthis 6c, Rhus Toxicodendron 6c, Bryonia Alba 6c
INCONTINENCE	Argentum Nitricum 6c, Causticum 30c, Conium Maculatum 30c, Pulsatilla 30c, Sepia 30c
INSECT BITES	Apis Mellifica 30c, Cantharis 30c, Hypericum Perforatum 6c, Urtica Urens 30c
ITCHING	Alumina 30c, Arsenicum Album 30c, Carbo Vegetabilis 30c, Hypericum Perforatum 6c, Mezerium 6c, Sulphur 30c
KENNEL COUGH	Drosera 6c, Ipecacuanha 30c
MASTITIS	Apis Mellifica 30c, Belladonna 30c, Urtica Urens 1m
PATELLAR LUXATION	Gelsemium Sempervirens 6c, Rhus Toxicodendron 6c
PENIS PROBLEMS	Aconitum Napellus 30c, Hepar Sulphuris Calcareum 30c, Pulsatilla 30c, Thuja Occidentalis 6c
PUPPY TEETHING	Calcarea Carbonica 6c, Chamomilla 6c, Phytolacca 6c
TRAVEL SICKNESS	Cocculus 6c, Petroleum 6c

Recognising a Sick Dog

Unlike colicky babies and cranky children, our canine charges cannot tell us when they are feeling ill. Therefore, there are a number of signs that owners can identify to know that their dogs are not feeling well.

Take note for physical manifestations such as:

- unusual, bad odour, including bad breath
- excessive moulting
- wax in the ears, chronic ear irritation
- oily, flaky, dull haircoat
- mucous, tearing or similar discharge in the eyes
- fleas or mites
- mucous in stool, diarrhoea
- sensitivity to petting or handling
- licking at paws, scratching face, etc.

Keep an eye out for behavioural changes as well including:

- lethargy, idleness
- lack of patience or general irritability
- lack of appetite, digestive problems
- phobias (fear of people, loud noises, etc.)
- strange behaviour, suspicion, fear
- coprophagia
- more frequent barking
- whimpering, crying

Get Well Soon

You don't need a DVR or a BVMA to provide good TLC to your sick or recovering dog, but you do need to pay attention to some details that normally wouldn't bother him. The following tips will aid Fido's recovery and get him back on his paws again:

- Keep his space free of irritating smells, like heavy perfumes and air fresheners.
- Rest is the best medicine! Avoid harsh lighting that will prevent your dog from sleeping. Shade him from bright sunlight during the day and dim the lights in the evening.
- Keep the noise level down. Animals are more sensitive to sound when they are sick.

- Be attentive to any necessary temperature adjustments. A dog with a fever needs a cool room and cold liquids. A bitch that is whelping or recovering from surgery will be more comfortable in a warm room, consuming warm liquids and food.
- You wouldn't send a sick child back to school early, so don't rush your dog back into a full routine until he seems absolutely ready.

Number-One Killer Disease in Dogs: CANCER

In every age there is a word associated with a disease or plague that causes humans to shudder. In the 21st century, that word is 'cancer.' Just as cancer is the leading cause of death in humans, it claims nearly half the lives of dogs that die from a natural disease as well as half the dogs that die over the age of ten years.

Described as a genetic disease, cancer becomes a greater risk as the dog ages. Veterinary surgeons and dog owners have become increasingly aware of the threat of cancer to dogs. Statistics reveal that one dog in every five will develop cancer, the most common of which is skin cancer. Many cancers, including prostate, ovarian and breast cancer, can be avoided by spaying and neutering our dogs by the age of six months.

Early detection of cancer can save or extend your dog's life, so it is absolutely vital for owners to have their dogs examined by a qualified veterinary surgeon or oncologist immediately upon detection of any abnormality. Certain dietary guidelines have also proven to reduce the onset and spread of cancer. Foods based on fish rather than beef, due to the presence of Omega-3 fatty acids, are recommended. Other amino acids such as glutamine have significant benefits for canines, particularly those breeds that show a greater susceptibility to cancer.

Cancer management and treatments promise hope for future generations of canines. Since the disease is genetic, breeders should never breed a dog whose parents, grandparents and any related siblings have developed cancer. It is difficult to know whether to exclude an otherwise healthy dog from a breeding programme as the disease does not manifest itself until the dog's senior years.

RECOGNISE CANCER WARNING SIGNS

Since early detection can possibly rescue your dog from becoming a cancer statistic, it is essential for owners to recognise the possible signs and seek the assistance of a qualified professional.

- Abnormal bumps or lumps that continue to grow
- Bleeding or discharge from any body cavity
- Persistent stiffness or lameness
- Recurrent sores or sores that do not heal
- Inappetence
- Breathing difficulties
- Weight loss
- Bad breath or odours
- General malaise and fatigue
- Eating and swallowing problems
- Difficulty urinating and defecating

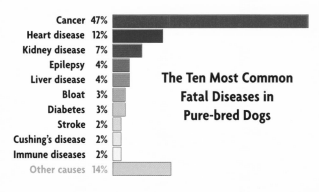

Cancer	47%
Heart disease	12%
Kidney disease	7%
Epilepsy	4%
Liver disease	4%
Bloat	3%
Diabetes	3%
Stroke	2%
Cushing's disease	2%
Immune diseases	2%
Other causes	14%

The Ten Most Common Fatal Diseases in Pure-bred Dogs

CDS: COGNITIVE DYSFUNCTION SYNDROME
'OLD-DOG SYNDROME'

There are many ways to evaluate old-dog syndrome. Veterinary surgeons have defined CDS (cognitive dysfunction syndrome) as the gradual deterioration of cognitive abilities. These are indicated by changes in the dog's behaviour. When a dog changes its routine response, and maladies have been eliminated as the cause of these behavioural changes, then CDS is the usual diagnosis.

More than half the dogs over eight years old suffer from some form of CDS. The older the dog, the more chance it has of suffering from CDS. In humans, doctors often dismiss the CDS behavioural changes as part of 'winding down.'

There are four major signs of CDS: the dog has frequent toilet accidents inside the home, sleeps much more or much less than normal, acts confused and fails to respond to social stimuli.

SYMPTOMS OF CDS

FREQUENT TOILET ACCIDENTS
- Urinates in the house.
- Defecates in the house.
- Doesn't signal that he wants to go out.

SLEEP PATTERNS
- Moves much more slowly.
- Sleeps more than normal during the day.
- Sleeps less during the night.

CONFUSION
- Goes outside and just stands there.
- Appears confused with a faraway look in his eyes.
- Hides more often.
- Doesn't recognise friends.
- Doesn't come when called.
- Walks around listlessly and without a destination.

FAILS TO RESPOND TO SOCIAL STIMULI
- Comes to people less frequently, whether called or not.
- Doesn't tolerate petting for more than a short time.
- Doesn't come to the door when you return home.

GERMAN SPITZ

The term *old* is a qualitative term. For dogs, as well as for their masters, old is relative. Certainly we can all distinguish between a puppy German Spitz and an adult German Spitz—there are the obvious physical traits, such as size, appearance and facial expressions, and personality traits. Puppies and young dogs like to play with children. Children's natural exuberance is a good match for the seemingly endless energy of young dogs. They like to run, jump, chase and retrieve. When dogs grow older and cease their interaction with children, they are often thought of as being too old to keep pace with the children. On the other hand, if a German Spitz is only exposed to older people or quieter lifestyles, his life will normally be less active and the decrease in his activity level as he ages will not be as obvious.

If people live to be 100 years old, dogs live to be 20 years old. While this might seem like a good rule of thumb, it is very inaccurate. When trying to compare dog years to human years, you cannot make a generalisation about all dogs. Thirteen years is roughly the average lifespan for the German Spitz, but, of course, there can be exceptions. Dogs generally are considered physically mature at three years of age (or earlier), but can reproduce even earlier. So the first three years of a dog's life are like seven times that of comparable humans. That means a 3-year-old dog is like a 21-year-old human. As the curve of comparison shows, there is no hard and fast rule for comparing dog and human ages. Small breeds tend to live longer than large breeds, some breeds' adolescent periods last longer than others' and some breeds experience rapid periods of growth. The comparison is made even more difficult, for, likewise, not all humans age at the same rate...and human females live longer than human males.

WHAT TO LOOK FOR IN SENIORS

Most veterinary surgeons and behaviourists use the seven-year mark as the time to consider a dog a 'senior' or 'veteran.' Neither term implies that the dog is geriatric and has begun to fail in mind and body. Ageing is essentially a slowing process. Humans readily admit that they feel a difference in their activity level from age 20 to 30, and then from 30 to 40, etc. By treating the seven-year-old dog as a senior, owners are able to implement certain therapeutic and preventative medical strategies with the help of their veterinary surgeons.

A senior-care programme should include at least two veterinary visits per year and screening sessions to determine the dog's health status, as well as nutritional counselling. Veterinary surgeons determine the senior dog's health status through a blood smear for a complete blood count, serum chemistry profile with electrolytes, urinalysis, blood pressure check, electrocardiogram, ocular tonometry (pressure on the eyeball) and dental prophylaxis.

Such an extensive programme for senior dogs is well advised before owners start to see the obvious physical signs of ageing, such as slower and inhibited movement, greying, increased sleep/nap periods and disinterest in play and other activity. This preventative programme promises a longer, healthier life for the ageing dog. Among the physical problems common in ageing dogs are the loss of sight and hearing, arthritis, kidney and liver failure, diabetes mellitus, heart disease and Cushing's disease (an hormonal disease).

In addition to the physical manifestations discussed, there

One of the first visible signs that a dog is getting older is greying around the muzzle.

are some behavioural changes and problems related to ageing dogs. Dogs suffering from hearing or vision loss, dental discomfort or arthritis can become aggressive. Likewise, the near-deaf and/or blind dog may be startled more easily and react in an unexpectedly aggressive manner. Seniors suffering from senility can become more impatient and irritable. Housesoiling accidents are associated with loss of mobility, kidney problems and loss of sphincter control as well as plaque accumulation, physiological brain changes and reactions to medications. Older dogs, just like young puppies, suffer from separation anxiety, which can lead to excessive barking, whining, housesoiling and destructive behaviour. Seniors may become fearful of everyday sounds, such as vacuum cleaners, heaters, thunder and passing traffic. Some dogs have difficulty sleeping, due to discomfort, the need for frequent toilet visits and the like.

Owners should avoid spoiling the older dog with too many fatty treats. Obesity is a common problem in older dogs and subtracts years from their lives. Keep the senior dog as trim as possible, since excess weight puts additional stress on the body's vital organs. Some breeders recommend supplementing the diet with foods high in fibre and lower in calories. Adding fresh vegetables and marrow broth to

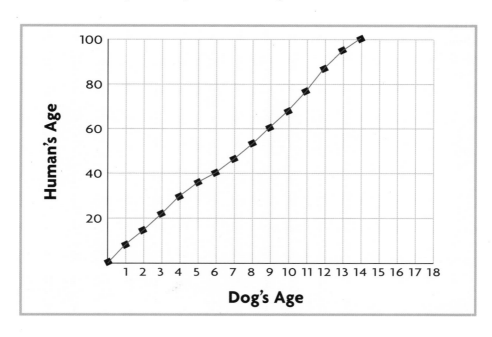

the senior's diet makes a tasty, low-calorie, low-fat supplement. Vets also offer speciality diets for senior dogs that are worth exploring.

Your dog, as he nears his twilight years, needs your patience and good care more than ever. Never punish an older dog for an accident or abnormal behaviour. For all the years of love, protection and companionship that your dog has provided, he deserves special attention and courtesies. The older dog may need to relieve himself at 3 a.m. because he can no longer hold it for eight hours. Older dogs may not be able to remain crated for more than two or three hours. It may be time to give up a sofa or chair to your old friend. Although he may not seem as enthusiastic about your attention and petting, he does appreciate the considerations you offer as he gets older.

Your German Spitz does not understand why his world is slowing down. Owners must make their dogs' transition into their golden years as pleasant and rewarding as possible.

WHAT TO DO WHEN THE TIME COMES

You are never fully prepared to make a rational decision about putting your dog to sleep. It is very obvious that you love your German Spitz or you would not be reading this book. Putting a

SENIOR SIGNS

An old dog starts to show one or more of the following symptoms:

- The hair on the face and paws starts to turn grey. The colour breakdown usually starts around the eyes and mouth.

- Sleep patterns are deeper and longer, and the old dog is harder to awaken.

- Food intake diminishes.

- Responses to calls, whistles and other signals are ignored more and more.

- Eye contact does not evoke tail wagging (assuming it once did).

beloved dog to sleep is extremely difficult. It is a decision that must be made with your veterinary surgeon. You are usually forced to make the decision when your dog experiences one or more life-threatening symptoms that have become serious enough for you to seek medical (veterinary) help.

If the prognosis of the malady indicates that the end is near and that your beloved pet will only continue to suffer and experience no enjoyment for the balance of its life, then euthanasia is the right choice.

WHAT IS EUTHANASIA?

Euthanasia derives from the Greek, meaning *good death*. In other words, it means the planned, painless killing of a dog suffering from a painful, incurable condition, or who is so aged that it cannot walk, see, eat or control its excretory functions. Euthanasia is usually accomplished by injection with an overdose of anaesthesia or a barbiturate. Aside from the prick of the needle, the experience is usually painless.

MAKING THE DECISION

The decision to euthanise your dog is never easy. The days during which the dog becomes ill and the end occurs can be unusually stressful for you. If this is your first experience with the death of a loved one, you may need the comfort dictated by your religious beliefs. If you are the head of the family and have children, you should have involved them in the decision of putting your German Spitz to sleep. Usually your dog can be maintained on drugs for a few days in order to give you ample time to make a decision. During this time, talking with members of your family or with people who have lived through the same experience can ease the burden of your inevitable decision.

THE FINAL RESTING PLACE

Dogs can have some of the same privileges as humans. The remains of your beloved dog can be buried in a pet cemetery, which is generally expensive. Alternatively, your dog can be cremated individually and the ashes returned to you. A less expensive option is mass cremation, although, of course, the ashes cannot then be returned. Vets can usually arrange the cremation on your behalf. The cost of these options should always be discussed frankly and

TALK IT OUT

The more openly your family discusses the whole stressful occurrence of the ageing and eventual loss of a beloved pet, the easier it will be for you when the time comes.

Many cities have pet cemeteries conveniently located. Your veterinary surgeon can assist you in locating one.

openly with your veterinary surgeon. In Britain, if your dog has died at the surgery, the vet legally cannot allow you to take your dog's body home as home burials are prohibited by law.

GETTING ANOTHER DOG?

The grief of losing your beloved dog will be as lasting as the grief of losing a human friend or relative. In most cases, if your dog died of old age (if there is such a thing), it had slowed down considerably. Do you want a new German Spitz puppy to replace it? Or are you better off finding a more mature German Spitz, say two to three years of age, which

will usually be house-trained and will have an already developed personality. In this case, you can find out if you like each other after a few hours of being together.

The decision is, of course, your own. Do you want another German Spitz or perhaps a different breed so as to avoid comparison with your beloved friend? Most people usually buy the same breed because they know (and love) the characteristics of that breed. Then, too, they often know people who have the same breed and perhaps they are lucky enough that one of their friends expects a litter soon. What could be better?

When you purchase your German Spitz, you will make it clear to the breeder whether you want one just as a loveable companion and pet, or if you hope to be buying a German Spitz with show prospects. No reputable breeder will sell you a young puppy and tell you that it is *definitely* of show quality, for so much can go wrong during the early months of a puppy's development. If you plan to show, what you will hopefully have acquired is a puppy with 'show potential.'

To the novice, exhibiting a German Spitz in the show ring may look easy, but it takes a lot of hard work and devotion to do top winning at a show such as the prestigious Crufts Dog Show, not to mention a little luck too!

The first concept that the canine novice learns when watching a dog show is that each dog first competes against members of its own breed. Once the judge has selected the best member of each breed (Best of Breed), provided that the show is judged on a Group system, that chosen dog will compete with other dogs in its group. Finally, the best of each group will compete for Best in Show.

The second concept that you must understand is that the dogs are not actually compared against one another. The judge compares each dog against its breed standard, which is the written description of the ideal specimen of the breed. While some early breed standards were indeed based on specific dogs that were famous or popular, many dedicated enthusiasts say that a perfect specimen, as described in the standard, has never walked into a show ring, has never been bred and, to the woe of dog breeders around the globe, does not exist. Breeders attempt to get as *close* to this ideal as possible with every litter, but theoretically the 'perfect' dog is so elusive that it is impossible. (And if the 'perfect' dog were born, breeders and judges probably would never agree that it was indeed 'perfect.')

If you are interested in exploring the world of dog showing, your best bet is to join your local breed club. These clubs often host both Championship and Open Shows, and sometimes Match meetings and special events, all of which could be of interest, even if you are only an onlooker. Clubs also send out newsletters, and some organise training days and seminars in order that people may learn more about their chosen breed. To locate the breed club closest to you, contact The Kennel Club, the ruling body for the British dog world.

The Kennel Club governs not only conformation shows but also working trials, obedience shows, agility trials and field trials. The Kennel Club furnishes the rules and regulations for all of these events plus general dog registration and other basic requirements of dog ownership. Its annual show, called the Crufts Dog Show, held in Birmingham, is the largest benched show in England. Every year over 20,000 of the UK's best dogs qualify to participate in this marvellous show, which lasts four days.

The Kennel Club governs many different kinds of shows in Great Britain, Australia, South Africa and beyond. At the most competitive and prestigious of these shows, the Championship Shows, a dog can earn Challenge Certificates (CCs), and thereby become a Show Champion or a Champion. A dog must earn three CCs under three different judges to earn the prefix of 'Sh Ch' or 'Ch.' Some breeds must also qualify in a field trial in order to gain the title of full Champion, though the German Spitz is not one such breed. CCs are awarded

Junior Handling is a great place to start for those youngsters interested in pursuing a career in the show ring.

to a very small percentage of the dogs competing, and dogs that are already Champions compete with others for these coveted CCs. The number of CCs awarded in any one year is based upon the total number of dogs in each breed entered for competition.

TYPES OF DOG SHOWS
There are three types of Championship Shows: an all-breed General Championship Show for all Kennel-Club-recognised breeds; a Group Championship Show, which is limited to breeds within one of the groups; and a Breed Show, which is usually confined to a single breed. The Kennel Club determines which breeds at which Championship Shows will have the opportunity to earn Challenge Certificates (or tickets). Serious exhibitors often will opt

not to participate if the tickets are withheld at a particular show. This policy makes earning championships even more difficult to accomplish.

Open Shows are generally less competitive and are frequently used as 'practice shows' for young dogs. There are hundreds of Open Shows each year, all of which can be delightful social events and are great first show experiences for the novice. Even if you're considering just watching a show to wet your paws, an Open Show is a great choice.

While Championship and Open Shows are most important for the beginner to understand, there are other types of shows in which the interested dog owner can participate. Training clubs sponsor Matches that can be entered on the day of the show for a nominal fee. In these introductory-level exhibitions, two dogs' names are pulled out of an hat and 'matched,' the winner of that match goes on to the next round and eventually only one dog is left undefeated.

Exemption Shows are much more light-hearted affairs with usually only four pedigree classes and several 'fun' classes, all of which can be entered on the day of the show. Exemption Shows are sometimes held in conjunction with small agricultural shows and the proceeds must be given to a charity. Limited Shows are also available in small number. Entry is restricted to members of the club that hosts the show, although one can usually join the club when making an entry.

ENTERING A DOG SHOW

Before you actually step into the ring, you would be well advised to sit back and observe the judge's ring procedure. If it is your first time in the ring, do not be over-anxious and run to the front of the line. It is much better to stand back and study how the exhibitor in front of you is performing. The judge asks each handler to 'stand' the dog, hopefully showing the dog off to his best advantage. The judge will observe the dog from a distance and from different angles, and approach the dog to check his teeth, overall structure, alertness and muscle tone, as well as consider how well the dog 'conforms' to the standard. Most importantly, the judge will have the exhibitor move the dog around the ring in some pattern that he or she should specify (another advantage to not going first, but always listen since some judges change their directions—and the judge is *always* right!). Finally, the judge will give the dog one last look before moving on to the next exhibitor.

If you are not in the top three at your first show, do not be discouraged. Be patient and consistent, and you may eventually find yourself in the winning line-up. Remember that the winners were once in your shoes and have devoted many hours and much money to earn the placement. If you find that your dog is losing every time and never getting a nod, it may be time to consider a different dog sport or to just enjoy your German Spitz as a pet.

Virtually all countries with a recognised speciality breed club (sometimes called a 'parent' club) offer show conformation competition specifically for and among German Spitz. Under direction of the club, other special events for hunting, tracking, obedience and agility may be offered as well, whether for titling or just for fun.

AGILITY TRIALS

Agility trials began in the United Kingdom in 1977 and have since spread around the world, especially to the United States, where they are very popular. The German Spitz's temperament is wonderful for agility, as this is a breed that loves to have fun! And while competitive, the focus in agility is on enjoyment. The German Spitz competes in mini-agility, in which the obstacles have been reduced in size to accommodate smaller breeds.

In an agility trial, the handler directs his dog over an obstacle

ON THE TABLE, PLEASE
In the show ring, German Spitzen are now measured on the judging table to see that they conform to the breed standard with regard to their height. People not familiar with measuring may be a little apprehensive about this, but it is surprising how quickly even a puppy gets used to the procedure. A competent judge can have the measuring stick on and off, almost in the blink of an eye!

course that includes jumps (such as those used in the working trials), as well as tyres, the dog walk, weave poles, pipe tunnels, collapsed tunnels, etc. The Kennel Club requires that dogs not be trained for agility until they are 12 months old. This dog sport is great fun for dog and owner, and interested owners should join a training club that has obstacles and experienced agility handlers who can introduce you and your dog to the 'ropes' (and tyres, tunnels, etc.).

FÉDÉRATION CYNOLOGIQUE INTERNATIONALE

Established in 1911, the Fédération Cynologique Internationale (FCI) represents the 'world kennel club.' This international body brings uniformity to the breeding, judging and showing of pure-bred dogs. Although the FCI originally included only five European nations: France, Germany, Austria, the Netherlands and Belgium (which remains its headquarters), the organisation today embraces nations on six continents and recognises well over 300 breeds of pure-bred dog.

FCI sponsors both national and international shows. The hosting country determines the judging system and breed standards are always based on the breed's country of origin. Dogs from every country can participate in these impressive canine spectacles, the largest of which is the World Dog Show, hosted in a different country each year.

There are three titles attainable through the FCI: the International Champion, which is the most prestigious; the International Beauty Champion, which is based on aptitude certificates in different countries; and the International Trial Champion, which is based on achievement in obedience trials in different countries. The top award in an FCI show is the CAC (*Certificat d'Aptitude au Championnat*) and to gain a championship, a dog must win three CACs at regional or club shows under three different judges who are breed specialists. The title of International Champion is gained by winning four CACIBs (*Certificats d'Aptitude au Championnat International de Beauté*), which are offered only at international shows, with at least a one-year lapse between the first and fourth award.

The FCI is divided into ten groups. At the World Dog Show, the following classes are offered for each breed: Puppy Class (6–9 months), Junior Class (9–18 months), Open Class (15 months or older) and Champion Class. A dog can be awarded a classification of Excellent, Very Good, Good, Sufficient and Not Sufficient. Puppies can be awarded classifications of Very Promising, Promising or Not Promising. Four placements are made in each class. After all classes are judged, a Best of Breed is selected. Other special groups and classes may also be shown. Each exhibitor showing a dog receives a written evaluation from the judge.

Behaviour of Your
GERMAN SPITZ

As a German Spitz owner, you have selected your dog so that you and your loved ones can have a companion, a watchdog, a friend and a four-legged family member. You invest time, money and effort to care for and train the family's new charge. Of course, this chosen canine behaves perfectly! Well, perfectly like a *dog*.

THINK LIKE A DOG
Dogs do not think like humans, nor do humans think like dogs, though we try. Unfortunately, a dog is incapable of compre-hending how humans think, so the responsibility falls on the owner to adopt a proper canine mindset. Dogs cannot rationalise, and they exist in the present moment. Many dog owners make the mistake in training of thinking that they can reprimand their dog for something he did a while ago. Basically, you cannot even reprimand a dog for something he did 20 seconds ago! Either catch him in the act or forget it! It is a waste of your and your dog's time—in his mind, you are reprimanding him for whatever he is doing at that moment.

The following behavioural problems represent those which

owners commonly encounter. Every dog is unique and every situation is unique. No author could purport for you to solve your German Spitz's problems simply by reading a script. Here we outline some basic 'dogspeak' so that owners' chances of solving behavioural problems are increased. Discuss bad habits with your veterinary surgeon and he can recommend a behavioural specialist to consult in appropriate cases. Since behavioural abnormalities are the main reason for owners' abandoning their pets, we hope that you will make a valiant effort to solve your German Spitz's problems. Patience and understanding are virtues that must dwell in every pet-loving household.

SEPARATION ANXIETY
Recognised by behaviourists as the most common form of stress for dogs, separation anxiety can also lead to destructive behav-iours in your dog. It's more than your German Spitz's howling his displeasure at your leaving the house and his being left alone. This is a normal reaction, no different from the child who cries

Dogs left at home all day on their own often become lonely, anxious and possibly destructive.

as his mother leaves him on the first day at school. Yet separation anxiety is more serious than this. In fact, if you are constantly with your dog, he will come to expect you with him all of the time, making it even more traumatic for him when you are not there.

Obviously, you enjoy spending time with your dog, and he thrives on your love and attention. However, it should not become a dependent relationship in which he is heartbroken without you. This broken heart can also bring on destructive behaviour as well as loss of appetite, depression and lack of interest in play and interaction. Canine behaviourists have been spending much time and energy to help owners better understand the significance of this stressful condition.

One thing you can do to minimise separation anxiety is to

make your entrances and exits as low-key as possible. Do not give your dog a long drawn-out goodbye, and do not lavish him with hugs and kisses when you return. This is giving in to the attention that he craves, and it will only make him miss it more when you are away. Another thing you can try is to give your dog a treat when you leave; this not only will keep him occupied and keep his mind off the fact that you have just left but it also will help him associate your leaving with a pleasant experience.

You may have to accustom your dog to being left alone in intervals. Of course, when your dog starts whimpering as you approach the door, your first instinct will be to run to him and comfort him, but do not do it! Really—eventually he will adjust to your absence. His anxiety stems from being placed in an unfam- iliar situation; by familiarising him with being alone, he will learn that he will survive. That is not to say you should purposely leave your dog home alone, but the dog needs to know that, while he can depend on you for his care, you do not have to be by his side 24 hours a day. Some behaviourists recommend tiring the dog out before you leave home—take him for a good long walk or engage in a game of fetch in the garden.

When the dog is alone in the

house, he should be placed in his crate—another distinct advantage to crate training your dog. The crate should be placed in his familiar happy family area, where he normally sleeps and already feels comfortable, thereby making him feel more at ease when he is alone. Be sure to give the dog a special chew toy to enjoy while he settles into his crate.

AGGRESSION

Although a good watchdog, the German Spitz is not an aggressive breed. The males remain non-aggressive even when a bitch is in season. Nonetheless, aggression is a concern for all responsible dog owners. Aggressive behaviour, when not controlled, always becomes dangerous. An aggressive dog, no matter the size, may lunge at, bite or even attack a person or another dog. Aggressive behaviour is not to be tolerated. It is more

I'M HOME!

Dogs left alone for varying lengths of time may often react wildly when their owners return. Sometimes they run, jump, bite, chew, tear things apart, wet themselves, gobble their food or behave in very undisciplined ways. If your dog behaves in this manner upon your return home, allow him to calm down before greeting him or he will consider your attention as a reward for his antics.

than just inappropriate behaviour; it is painful for a family to watch their dog become unpredictable in his behaviour to the point where they are afraid of him. While not all aggressive behaviour is dangerous, growling, baring teeth, etc. can be frightening.

It is important to ascertain why the dog is acting in this manner. Aggression is a display of dominance, and the dog should not have the dominant role in his pack, which is, in this case, your family.

Fear is a common cause of aggression in dogs. Perhaps your German Spitz had a negative experience as a puppy, which causes him to be fearful when a similar situation presents itself later in life. The dog may act aggressively in order to protect himself from whatever is making him afraid. It is not always easy to determine what is making your dog fearful, but if you can isolate what brings out the fear reaction, you can help the dog get over it.

Supervise your German Spitz's interactions with people and other dogs, and praise the dog when it goes well. If he starts to act aggressively in a situation, correct him and remove him from the situation. Do not let people approach the dog and start petting him without your express permission. That way, you can have the dog sit to accept petting, and praise him when he behaves properly. You are focusing on praise and on modifying his behaviour by rewarding him when he acts appropriately. By being gentle and by supervising his interactions, you are showing him that there is no need to be afraid or defensive.

In the rare case of an aggressive German Spitz, the best solution is to consult a behavioural specialist, one who has experience with the breed if possible. Together, perhaps you can pinpoint the cause of your dog's aggression and rectify the situation before it becomes serious.

SEXUAL BEHAVIOUR

Dogs exhibit certain sexual behaviours that may have influenced your choice of male or female when you first purchased your German Spitz. To a certain extent, spaying/neutering may eliminate these behaviours, but if you are purchasing a dog that you wish to breed from, you should be aware of what you will have to deal with throughout the dog's life.

Female dogs usually have two oestruses per year, with each season lasting about three weeks. These are the only times in which a female dog will mate, and she usually will not allow this until the second week of the cycle, although this varies from bitch to bitch. If not bred during the heat cycle, it is not uncommon for a bitch to experience a false pregnancy, in which her mammary glands swell and she exhibits maternal tendencies toward toys or other objects.

With male dogs, owners must be aware that whole dogs (dogs who are not neutered) have the natural inclination to mark their territory. Males mark their territory by spraying small amounts of urine as they lift their legs in a macho ritual. Marking can occur both outdoors in the garden and around the neighbourhood as well as indoors on furniture legs, curtains and the sofa. Such behaviour can be very frustrating for the owner; early training is strongly urged before the 'urge' strikes your dog. Neutering the male at an appropriate early age can solve this problem before it becomes an habit.

Other problems associated with males are wandering and mounting. Both of these habits, of course, belong to the unneutered dog, whose sexual drive leads him away from home in search of the bitch in heat. Males will mount females in heat, as well as any other dog, male or female, that happens to catch their fancy. Other possible mounting partners include his owner, the furniture, guests to the home and strangers on the street. Discourage such behaviour early on.

Owners must further recognise that mounting is not merely a sexual expression but also one of dominance seen in males and females alike. Be consistent and be persistent, and you will find that you can 'move mounters.'

CHEWING

The national canine pastime is chewing! Every dog loves to sink his 'canines' into a tasty bone, but sometimes that bone is in his owner's hand! Dogs need to chew, to massage their gums, to make their new teeth feel better and to exercise their jaws. Though German Spitzen are not known especially as chewers, chewing is a natural behaviour that is deeply embedded in all things canine. Our role as owners is not to stop the dog's chewing, but rather to redirect it to positive, chew-worthy objects. Be an informed owner and purchase proper chew toys, like strong nylon bones, that will not splinter. Be sure that the objects are safe and durable, since your dog's safety is at risk. Again, the owner is responsible for ensuring a dog-proof environment.

The best answer is prevention; that is, put your shoes, handbags and other tasty objects in their proper places (out of the reach of the growing canine mouth). Direct puppies to their toys whenever you see them 'tasting' the

Chewing is an instinctive behaviour in dogs. If your German Spitz chews on something inappropriate, you are to blame...either for lack of supervision or for not providing proper chew toys.

furniture legs or the leg of your trousers. Make a loud noise to attract the pup's attention and immediately escort him to his chew toy and engage him with the toy for at least four minutes, praising and encouraging him all the while. An array of safe, interesting chew toys will keep your dog's mind and teeth occupied, and distracted from chewing on things he shouldn't.

Some trainers recommend deterrents, such as hot pepper, a bitter spice or a product designed for this purpose, to discourage the dog from chewing unwanted objects. Test these products to see which works best before investing in large quantities.

BARKING

Dogs cannot talk—oh, what they would say if they could! Instead, barking is a dog's way of 'talking.' It can be somewhat frustrating because it is not always easy to tell what a dog means by his bark—is he excited, happy, frightened or angry? Whatever it is that the dog is trying to say, he should not be punished for barking. It is only when the barking becomes excessive, and when the excessive barking becomes a bad habit, that the behaviour needs to be modified.

The German Spitz is a good watchdog, and will bark in new situations or when apprehensive about something. Fortunately, German Spitzen tend to use their barks more purposefully than do many other breeds. For example, if an intruder came into your home in the middle of the night and your German Spitz barked a warning, wouldn't you be pleased? You would probably deem your dog an hero, a wonderful guardian and protector of the home. On the other hand, if a friend drops by unexpectedly, rings the doorbell and is greeted with a sudden sharp bark, you would probably be annoyed at the dog. But in reality, isn't this just the same behaviour? The dog does not know any better. Unless he sees who is at the door and it is someone he knows, he will bark as a means of vocalising that his (and your) territory is being threatened. While your friend is not posing a threat, it is all the same to the dog. Barking is his means of letting you know that there is an intrusion, whether friend or foe, on your property. This type of barking is instinctive and should not be discouraged.

Excessive habitual barking, however, is a problem that should be corrected early on. As your German Spitz grows up, you will be able to tell when his barking is purposeful and when it is for no reason. You will become able to distinguish your dog's different barks and their meanings. For example, the bark when someone comes to the door will be different from the bark when he is excited to see you. It is similar to a person's tone of voice, except that the dog has to rely totally on tone of voice because he does not have the benefit of using words. An incessant barker will be evident at an early age.

There are some things that encourage a dog to bark. For example, if your dog barks non-stop for a few minutes and you give him a treat to quieten him, he believes that you are rewarding him for barking. He will associate barking with getting a treat and will keep doing it until he is rewarded. On the other hand, if you give him a command such as 'Quiet' and praise him after he has stopped barking for a few seconds, he will get the idea that being 'quiet' is what you want him to do.

JUMPING UP

Jumping up is a dog's friendly way of saying hello! Some dog owners do not mind when their dog jumps up. The problem arises when guests come to the house and the dog greets them in the same manner—whether they like it or not! However friendly the greeting may be, chances are that your visitors will not appreciate your dog's enthusiasm. The dog will not be able to distinguish upon whom he can jump and whom he cannot. Therefore, it is probably best to discourage this behaviour entirely.

Pick a command such as 'Off' (avoid using 'Down' since you will use that for the dog to lie down) and tell him 'Off' when he jumps up. Place him on the ground on all fours and have him sit, praising him the whole time. Always lavish him with praise and petting when he is in the sit position. In this way, you can give him a warm affectionate greeting, let him know that you are as excited to see him as he is to see you and instil good manners at the same time!

DIGGING

Digging, which is seen as a destructive behaviour to humans, is actually quite a natural behaviour in dogs. Although terriers (the 'earth dogs') are most associated with the digging, any dog's desire to dig can be irrepressible and most frustrating to his owners. When digging occurs in your garden, it is actually a normal behaviour redirected into something the dog can do in his everyday life. In the wild, a dog would be actively seeking food, making his own shelter, etc. He would be using his paws in a purposeful manner for his survival. Since you provide him with food and shelter, he has no need to use his paws for these purposes, and so the energy that he would be using may manifest itself in the form of little holes all over your garden and flower beds.

German Spitzen are not generally known to be diggers, so perhaps your dog is digging as a reaction to boredom. It is some- what similar to someone's eating a whole bag of crisps in front of the TV—because they are there and

It's not only the 'earth dogs' that dig. Any dog, puppy or adult, may have an inclination to getting his paws dirty.

there is nothing better to do! Basically, the answer is to provide the dog with adequate play and exercise so that his mind and paws are occupied, and so that he feels as if he is doing something useful.

Of course, digging is easiest to control if it is stopped as soon as possible, but it is often hard to catch a dog in the act. If your dog is a compulsive digger and is not easily distracted by other activities, you can designate an area on your property where he is allowed to dig. If you catch him digging in an off-limits area of the garden, immediately bring him to the approved area and praise him for digging there. Keep a close eye on him so that you can catch him in the act—that is the only way to make him understand what is permitted and what is not. If you take him to an hole he dug an hour ago and tell him 'No,' he will understand that you are not fond of holes, or dirt or flowers. If you catch him while he is stifle-deep in your tulips, that is when he will get your message.

FOOD STEALING

Is your dog devising ways of stealing food from your coffee table or cupboard? If so, you must answer the following questions: Is your German Spitz hungry, or is he 'constantly famished' like many dogs seem to be? Face it, some dogs are more food-

> ### AIN'T MISBEHAVING
> Punishment is rarely necessary for a misbehaving dog. Dogs that habitually behave badly probably had a poor education and do not know what is expected of them. They need training. Negative reinforcement on your part usually does more harm than good.

motivated than others. They are totally obsessed by the smell of food and can only think of their next meal. Food stealing is terrific fun and always yields a great reward—FOOD, glorious food.

Your goal as an owner, therefore, is to be sensible about where food is placed in the home and to reprimand your dog whenever he is caught in the act of stealing. But remember, only reprimand your dog if you actually see him stealing, not later when the crime is discovered; that will be of no use at all and will only serve to confuse him.

BEGGING

Just like food stealing, begging is a favourite pastime of hungry puppies! It achieves that same lovely result—FOOD! Dogs quickly learn that their owners keep the 'good food' for themselves, and that we humans do not dine on dried food alone. Begging is a conditioned response related to a specific stimulus, time and place. The sounds of the kitchen, cans and bottles opening, crinkling bags, the smell of food in preparation, etc. will excite the dog, and soon the paws will be in the air!

Here is the solution to stopping this behaviour: Never give in to a beggar! You are rewarding the dog for sitting pretty, jumping up, whining and rubbing his nose into you by giving him food. By ignoring the dog, you will (eventually) force the behaviour into extinction. Note that the behaviour is likely to get worse before it disappears, so be sure there are not any 'softies' in the family who will give in to little 'Oliver' every time he whimpers, 'More, please.'

COPROPHAGIA

Faeces eating is, to humans, one of the most disgusting behaviours that their dogs could engage in, yet, to dogs, it is perfectly normal. It is hard for us to understand why a dog would want to eat his own faeces. He could be seeking certain nutrients that are missing from his diet, he could be just plain hungry or he could be attracted by the pleasing (to a dog) scent. While coprophagia most often refers to the dog's eating his own faeces, a dog may just as likely eat that of another animal as well if he comes across it. Dogs often find the stool of cats and horses more palatable than that of other dogs.

Vets have found that diets with low levels of digestibility, containing relatively low levels of fibre and high levels of starch, increase coprophagia. Therefore, high-fibre diets may decrease the likelihood of dogs' eating faeces. Both the consistency of the stool (how firm it feels in the dog's mouth) and the presence of undigested nutrients increase the likelihood. Once the dog develops diarrhoea from faeces eating, he will likely stop this distasteful habit.

To discourage this behaviour, first make sure that the food you are feeding your dog is nutritionally complete and that he is getting enough food. If changes in his diet do not seem to work, and no medical cause can be found, you will have to modify the behaviour through environmental control before it becomes an habit. The best way to prevent your dog from eating his stool is to make it unavailable—clean up after he eliminates and remove any stool from the garden. If it is not there, he cannot eat it.

Reprimanding for stool eating rarely impresses the dog. Vets recommend distracting the dog while he is in the act of stool eating. Coprophagia is seen most frequently in pups 6 to 12 months of age, and usually disappears around the dog's first birthday.

INDEX

My German Spitz

PUT YOUR PUPPY'S FIRST PICTURE HERE

Dog's Name _____

Date _____ Photographer _____